THE TRANSFORMATION
OF MEDIEVAL ENGLAND

1370–1529

General editor: *Geoffrey Holmes*

THE TRANSFORMATION OF MEDIEVAL ENGLAND
1370–1529
John A. F. Thomson

THE EMERGENCE OF A NATION STATE
The commonwealth of England 1529–1660
Alan G. R. Smith

THE MAKING OF A GREAT POWER
Late Stuart and Early Georgian Britain 1660–1722
Geoffrey Holmes

THE AGE OF OLIGARCHY
Pre-Industrial Britain 1722–1783
Geoffrey Holmes and Daniel Szechi

THE FORGING OF THE MODERN STATE
Early industrial Britain 1783–1870
Eric J. Evans

THE ECLIPSE OF A GREAT POWER
Modern Britain 1870–1992
Second Edition
Keith Robbins

THE TRANSFORMATION OF MEDIEVAL ENGLAND
1370–1529

John A. F. Thomson

LONGMAN
LONDON AND NEW YORK

Longman Group Limited
Longman House, Burnt Mill, Harlow
Essex CM20 2JE, England
and Associated Companies throughout the world.

*Published in the United States of America
by Longman Publishing, New York*

First published 1983
Sixth impression 1995

British Library Cataloguing in Publication Data
Thomson, John A. F.
  The transformation of medieval England
  1370 – 1529 – (Foundations of modern Britain)
  1. Great Britain – History – 14th century
  2. Great Britain – History – Tudors, 1485–1603
  I. Title   II. Series
  942   DA225

ISBN 0-582-48976-8

Library of Congress Cataloging in Pulication Data
Thomson, John A. F.
  The transformation of medieval England, 1370–1529.

  (Foundations of modern Britain)
  Bibliography: p.
  Includes index.
    1. Great Britain – History – Medieval period,
  1066 – 1485. 2. Great Britain – History – Tudors. 1485 – 1603.
  I. Title   II. Series.
  DA175.T45   942.04   82 – 15336
  ISBN 0-582-48975-X   AACR2
  ISBN 0-582-48976-8 (pbk.)

Set in linotron 202 Times
Produced by Longman Singapore Publishers Pte Ltd
Printed in Singapore.

Contents

Contents

List of maps

Editor's foreword

So prodigious has been the output of specialized work on British history during the past twenty years, and so rich its diversity, that scholars and students thirst continually after fresh syntheses. Even those who read for the pure pleasure of informing themselves about the past have become quite reconciled to the fact that little can now be taken for granted. An absorbing interest in local situations, as a way to understanding more general ones; a concern with those processes of social change which accompany economic, educational and cultural development, and which often condition political activity too: these and many other strong currents of modern historiography have washed away some of our more comfortable orthodoxies. Even when we know *what* happened, there is endless scope for debate about *why* things happened and with what consequences.

In such circumstances a new series of general textbooks on British history would not seem to call for elaborate justification. However, the six volumes constituting *Foundations of Modern Britain* do have a distinct rationale and they embody some novel features. For one thing, they make a serious attempt to present a history of Britain from the point at which 'Britain' became first a recognizable entity and then a great power, and to trace the foundations of this State in the history of pre-eighteenth-century England. The fact that five of the six authors either have taught or are teaching in Scottish universities, while one has held a chair in the University of Wales, should at least help to remind them that one aim of the series is to avoid excessive Anglo-centricity. The first two volumes, spanning the years 1370–1660, will certainly concentrate primarily on the history of England, emphasizing those developments which first prepared the way for, and later confirmed her emergence as an independent 'commonwealth', free from Continental trammels whether territorial or ecclesiastical. But the reader should also be aware, as he reads them, of England's ultimate role as the heart of a wider island kingdom in which men of three nations came to be associated. During the period covered by volumes 3, 4 and 5 1660–1870, this 'United Kingdom of Great Britain' became not only a domestic reality but the centre of an Empire and the posssessor of world-wide influence. Space will allow only limited treatment of Ireland and of Anglo-Irish relations until after the Union of 1801. It is appropriate, however, that in the final volume of the series reasserted nationalism should figure almost as strongly as the erosion of imperial status in the story of Britain's slide down the slippery slope from palmy greatness to anxious mediocrity. The original terminal date of volume 6, 1975, was deliberately chosen: the year in which Britain, tortured once again by her Irish inheritance and facing demands for Scottish devolution, or even independence, belatedly recognized that the days of complacent self-sufficiency as regards Europe, too, were past.

As well as paying more than mere lip-service to its own title, the present series adopts an irreverent attitude to time-honoured chronological divisions. Those lines of demarcation between volumes which dominated virtually every English history series conceived before 1960 (and, with a few exceptions, have displayed a remarkable capacity for survival subsequently) are seen as a quite unnecessary obstacle to readers' understanding of the way modern historiography has reshaped whole vistas of our island's history in the past forty years. Years such as 1485, 1603, 1689, 1714, 1760 or 1815 established themselves in textbook lore at a time when they accurately reflected the heavily political and constitutional emphasis of traditional history teaching. Even on those terms they have become of limited utility. But equally seriously, the conventions which such divisions perpetuate often make it extremely difficult for authors to accommodate fundamental aspects of social and economic development within their allotted compass. The brutal slicing off of 'Tawney's century' (1540–1640) at 1603 is perhaps the worst of these atrocities; but it is not the only one.

All dates are to some extent arbitrary as lines of division, and all present their own difficulties. It is hoped, none the less, that those selected in this series to enclose periods which are in any case a good deal longer than average, may prove less inhibiting and confusing than some of their predecessors and much more adaptable to the needs of British history courses in Universities and colleges.

In one further important respect the authors have kept in mind the practical requirements of students and teachers. Their approach eschews lengthy narrative wherever possible and concentrates, within chapters short enough to be rapidly absorbed, on the development of themes and the discussion of problems. Yet at the same time they attempt to satisfy their readers' need for basic information in two ways: by providing, at appropriate stages, skeletal 'frameworks' of events, chronologically ordered, within which the subsequent analysis and interplay of argument can be set; and by placing at the end of each volume a 'compendium' of factual data, including statistics, on a scale much greater than that of normal textbook appendices.

These compendia are essential companions to the texts and are designed for ready and constant use. The frequent references to them which punctuate so many chapters in this series will be found within square brackets, for example thus [B.2]. They should be easily distinguishable from the numerous arabic numbers within round brackets inserted in each text, e.g. (117). These refer readers to the Bibliography, in which most items are thematically arranged and serially numbered. Superior numerals are for the notes which are listed at the ends of chapters.

Geoffrey Holmes

Preface

In the course of writing this book I have incurred many debts of gratitude which it is a pleasure to acknowledge. The authorship of a textbook compels one to study topics where one cannot claim real expertise and teaches one forcibly how much one must depend on the labours of others, who have done the basic research. My first debt, therefore, is to the scholars whose work I have used, some living, some dead, some known to me but many more who are strangers. The names of some are acknowledged in the bibliography, but equal thanks are due to many others who could not be mentioned because of limitations of space.

Secondly, thanks are due to those who gave more immediate assistance in the preparation of the work. Dr. Alan Smith and Dr. Michael Clanchy gave me the benefit of their specialist knowledge in particular chapters, and the general editor of the series, Professor Geoffrey Holmes scrutinized the text meticulously and made many useful suggestions for improving it. My wife suggested various improvements to the text to eliminate ambiguities in the argument and infelicities in the style, and she and my son helped in the preparation of the index. Miss Mary Brodie prepared the typescript for the publishers, dealing successfully with various drafts of it, and the staff of Longman have given support throughout the period of writing by being willing to come more than half way to meet the wishes of the author.

Finally, my greatest debt is to my colleagues and students in the History department of the University of Glasgow, in discussion with whom during the last twenty years so many of the ideas in this book were originally formulated. Their comments and questions have often forced me to rethink my views on particular problems of the period or to justify more fully views which I already held. The book is dedicated to Professor Lionel Stones, who originally appointed me to the department. His stress on the values of material as well as documentary sources for history has given me new perspectives on the subject, and his friendship and encouragement has always helped me in my work.

John A. F. Thomson

Acknowledgements

We are grateful to the following for permission to reproduce copyright material:

London School of Economics and Political Science for our table A.1 from 'Index of Prices and Wages' by H. Phelps Brown and S. Hopkins *Economica* pp 311–2, November 1956; Oxford University Press for our table A.2 (E. M. Carus-Wilson & O. Coleman 1963).

Prologue. England in 1370

On 3 June 1369 Edward III resumed the title of King of France which he had abandoned in 1360 under the terms of the Treaty of Brétigny. This action was prompted by the claim of the Valois King Charles V that he was entitled to hear appeals from the Gascon lands held by the English King. In November, the French King retaliated by declaring these lands confiscated, and the Anglo-French War was renewed. The prominence of this war in English fourteenth-century history reveals very clearly the orientation of royal policy towards western Europe. For the greater part of his reign, Edward had been largely preoccupied with defending the lands which he had inherited in south-west France, something which had been true, at any rate for part of the time, of his father and grandfather also. Indeed ever since 1066, the English crown had had territorial interests in France. During the war Edward had himself laid claim, on somewhat dubious grounds, to the French throne itself, and his military victories before 1360 had led to a large increase in the territory which was either directly under his control or ruled by men who recognized his feudal superiority. In 1360, he held the greater part of western France south of the Loire, and his eldest son, the Black Prince, had a court of his own at Bordeaux.

It is hardly surprising, therefore, that the King's mental world, and that of his closest associates, was not bounded by the English Channel. It was that of the international chivalric class, whose achievements were celebrated in the chronicle of the Hainaulter Jean Froissart, and whose prominent members were equally at home in England and on the Continent. Indeed another Hainaulter, Sir Walter Manny, was a much respected member of Edward's court, and one of the earliest knights of the King's new Order of the Garter. For such men, French was their natural tongue, as is shown by the fact that when Henry of Grosmont, duke of Lancaster and a noted war captain, wrote a religious treatise, *Le Livre de Seyntz Medecines*, this was the language which he employed. By the late fourteenth century, however, one can see signs of a decline in this employment of French and the appearance of a strong vernacular literature in writers such as Langland and Chaucer. The use of English by the latter writer, who had close connections with the court, is particularly significant as a sign of the progress of English in polite society, although one must remember that much of his writing was in a cosmopolitan European tradition in both subject and form. An equally important sign of the progress of English was the abandonment of French in some classes of official document, such as the complaints presented by Convocation to Parliament, although there were places where it was firmly rooted, notably in the conservative atmosphere of the law courts. It is likely that this widespread decline in the use of French was connected with the hostility engendered by war and its accompanying propaganda. The result was that English, for the first time in over three centuries, was becoming respectable in the upper levels of society; it was also spreading as a cultural medium below court level, and was coming to be taught in schools.

One area in which the vernacular had already become well established in the fourteenth century was in religious literature; it was almost certainly the social background of Henry of Grosmont that had led him to choose French for his book, as works which were directed to an audience lower in the social scale were already being written in English. Although the Church represented an international culture, the appearance of vernacular writings was not a peculiarly English phenomenon but may be paralleled elsewhere in Christendom, as literacy spread increasingly throughout a substantial part of lay society. The writing of vernacular sermons and the appearance of such works as *The Cloud of Unknowing* and the English writings of Richard Rolle reflect attempts to fill a gap in the spiritual life of a people who were concerned with ultimate values but who could not share the Latin culture of churchmen. Such progress in learning counted for far more in developing a national religious literature than any political factors, although it is also true that the tendency of the Church to centralization, manifest since the eleventh century, was coming under increasing strain. The suspicion that French-born popes at Avignon were politically antagonistic exacerbated resentment at papal intervention in the affairs of the English Church, and in the middle years of Edward III's reign steps were taken to curtail it. These moves were purely political and administrative, for in 1370 English religious life was strongly orthodox, and gave little indication that it was soon to be affected by a major heretical movement. The spread of devotional writings from their traditional environment in the monasteries was the only sign of how popular feeling could not be contained within its traditional limits.

There is little doubt that the country over which Edward had ruled for about forty years, and which was increasingly developing this national consciousness, was politically and economically powerful. This is clearly revealed by its successes in war against its larger neighbour France, and its limitation of the lesser threat from France's ally, Scotland. By 1370, he had abandoned attempts to dominate Scotland through a puppet ruler, but he had secured effective authority in Wales and was trying to strengthen his position in Ireland. Politically, the King made a considerable personal contribution to his country's achievements, most notably in the way in which, for most of his reign, he maintained friendly relations with the magnate class. This contrasts markedly with the unhappy experience of his father's time, when Crown and nobility had been constantly at loggerheads. One reason for this was certainly that he conformed in his life and attitudes to the ideal of kingship which was held by the magnates in a way in which his father had not, another was that he was well served in administrative matters by his principal ministers. These were still normally churchmen, although by the late fourteenth century, legally trained laymen had occasionally held important offices of State, and were encroaching on the earlier clerical monopoly of them. The King's administrators were able to mobilize effectively the nation's resources for war, and the magnate admiration for the King's military success was due as much to this as to Edward's capacity as a strategist or a tactician.

War taxation, however, also contributed to the consolidation of the nation's political identity, because the King's need for money led him to have increasingly frequent recourse to Parliament for grants, and it was during this period of war that Parliament became the effective paymaster to meet the King's needs. In 1362, it was agreed that no tax on wool should be granted by merchants or others without the consent of Parliament (53, p.161). This prevented the King from negotiating separately with any other body in the State, and by 1370 Parliament was the principal point of communication between the King and his subjects. It was still dominated by the great men who received individual writs of summons to its meetings, the future House of Lords, but the representatives of the shires and boroughs were becoming increasingly willing to voice criticisms of abuses in government and to resist taxation if they regarded it as excessive.

One of the major sources of such taxation was the levy of export duties on wool, a fact which is a reminder that the strength of the English economy rested on the country's production of raw materials rather than of manufactured goods. English wool was supplied to the looms of Flanders and Italy and was highly regarded in those countries. Politics and economics were particularly closely interrelated in Anglo-Flemish relations, because of the geographical and strategic situation of Flanders in the French War, and when in 1369 the heiress to the county married a younger brother of Charles V, Philip, duke of Burgundy, the possibility of applying economic sanctions became even more crucial. The economy of western Europe had in the earlier part of the century been affected seriously by factors beyond human control – famine between 1315 and 1317, and from the middle of the century the Black Death and subsequent epidemics. These obviously affected England also, although it is hard to judge their immediate effects. The initial effects of pestilence were not so great as to curtail the King's military activities in the 1350s, but there are signs that by 1370 the long-term effects of population decline, from an earlier peak between 4½ and 6 million, were causing some dislocation of the traditional types of manorial organization and affecting the resources of the magnate class. While it would be wrong to suggest that manorialism had remained static in character in the years before 1350, it is probably correct to say that the earlier changes were prompted by the attempts of the landowners, who held the whip-hand, to exploit their resources more fully. The balance of power between the manorial lord and his subordinates, both tenants and employed labourers, was, however, decisively upset by the labour shortage, and by 1370 the land-owning class was on the defensive. The main developments in the late-fourteenth-century economy resulted primarily from pressures from below for improved conditions in both economic and legal terms. Most notably, one can see the difficulties faced by the magnates and gentry in trying to assert their old legal rights over men who had formerly been unfree. The power of the lords had not yet been significantly reduced by 1370, and a substantial number of their men had not yet secured legal freedom, but the land-owners were having increasing problems in maintaining their old rights.

Outside manorial society, urban life had developed less fully in England than on the Continent, but London was already a great metropolis, more comparable with some of the cities of western Europe than with any other English town. With a population of probably between 30,000 and 40,000, it was more than three times the size of the next largest English towns, York and Bristol. Other major provincial centres were Norwich and Coventry, both of which had well under 10,000 inhabitants (104, p.1). London's dominance rested on a combination of factors, particularly its position near the centre of government in adjacent Westminster and its favourable geographical situation in relation to English Continental trade. The ruling mercantile group in London was perhaps the most important body of men in the country after the landed aristocracy and the higher clergy. Leading London merchants, particularly the city mayor, could play a prominent part in national politics and normally dominated England's trade with the Low Countries and northern Europe. The prominence of the Londoners was all the more marked when one sees that in general the merchant class took a very clear second place behind the landowners, nowhere more marked than in Parliament where the burgesses played only a supporting role to the more influential knights of the shire.

The renewal of the war was to lead to the revival of various tensions in English society in the 1370s. The need for war taxation gave rise to fiscal difficulties, and as the King aged he could no longer provide the kind of leadership which had carried him through the early stages of the struggle with France. The harmonious relations which had existed between the King and his subjects for over a generation were breaking down through a combination of economic problems and lack of leadership at the top.

PART ONE

Environment and economy

In the case of major epidemics, it is often impossible to specify their nature in detail, as contemporary records are often imprecise. The term 'plague' may denote an epidemic of bubonic or pneumonic plague, but it may also be used more generally to describe any pestilence. Also it is not clear what was the nature of the disease known as the 'sweating sickness'. In the table below the less precise term 'epidemic' is normally employed, rather than anything more precise, because the economic consequences of such outbreaks resulted from the fact that they occurred, not from their particular nature. It is impossible to state how widespread such epidemics were; many of those in the fifteenth century seem to have been particularly severe in London; on a number of occasions our knowledge of an outbreak depends on the fact that the meeting of Parliament was adjourned to a location in the provinces to avoid danger to those attending it.

Entries in *italics* refer to political events and have been included to provide a cross-reference to the Framework of events – Political.

1348–49	Initial attack of the Black Death.
1361–62	Epidemic.
1369	Epidemic. *Renewal of Anglo-French War.*
1373	Bristol granted legal status as a county.
1375	Epidemic.
1377	*Succession of Richard II.*
1381	Great Revolt. Main centres of disorder in Kent, Essex, East Anglia, Cambridgeshire, Hertfordshire, London. Isolated outbreaks in Bedfordshire, Buckinghamshire, Cheshire, Leicestershire, Northamptonshire, Somerset, Warwickshire, Yorkshire.
1385–88	Tension between England and the Hanse towns.
1387–88	*Revolt of the Lords Appellant against Richard II.*
1389	*Truce with France.*
1390	Epidemic.
1392–97	London lost municipal autonomy.
1396	York granted legal status as a county. *Twenty-eight-year truce with France.*
1399	*Succession of Henry IV.*
1400	Newcastle granted legal status as a county.
1404	Norwich granted legal status as a county.
1405–8	Tension between England and the Hanse towns.
1405	Epidemic.
1409	Lincoln granted legal status as a county.
1413	Epidemic. *Succession of Henry V.*
1415	*Renewal of war in France.*
1422	*Succession of Henry VI.*
1431	Rising at Abingdon, Berkshire. Supposedly Lollard, but little evidence of heresy. Trouble also in Wiltshire, Coventry and London.
1431–37	Tension between England and the Hanse towns.
1433	Epidemic.
1434	Epidemic.
1435	*Congress of Arras; Burgundian change of sides in war.*
1437	Epidemic.
1438–39	Food shortages after bad harvest.
1439	Epidemic. Peace settlement and trade agreement with Burgundy.

1440	Hull granted perpetual succession as a legal personality.
1444	Epidemic.
1446	Robert Sturmy of Bristol sent ship, the cog *Anne*, into the Mediterranean.
1448–50	Epidemics.
1449–56	Tension between England and the Hanse towns.
1450	*Loss of Normandy.* Cade's rising in Kent. Disorders in Wiltshire at the same time. Trouble persisted in Kent for two more years on a less widespread scale.
1452	Epidemic.
1453	*Final expulsion of the English from France.*
1454	Epidemic.
1457	Robert Sturmy sent ship, *Katherine*, into the Mediterranean.
1461	*Succession of Edward IV.*
1464	Epidemic. Reduction in bullion value of coinage.
1468–75	Tension between England and the Hanse towns.
1470–1	*Readeption of Henry VI.*
1471	Epidemic. During Lancastrian attack on London, Essex men with economic grievances joined Fauconberg's Kentishmen.
1475	Trade treaty with Hanse towns.
1479	Epidemic.
1480s	Search for 'island of Brasil' by ships from Bristol.
1483	*Succession of Edward V. Usurpation of Richard III.*
1485	Epidemic. *Succession of Henry VII.*
1486	Trade treaties with Brittany and France.
1489	Anti-tax revolt in Yorkshire. Murder of the earl of Northumberland.
1493	Epidemic.
1496	Trade treaty with Low Countries (*Intercursus Magnus*).
1497	John Cabot, voyaging out of Bristol, reached Newfoundland. Trade treaty with France. Cornish revolt and march on London.
1499–1500	Epidemic.
1505	Epidemic.
1509	*Succession of Henry VIII.*
1521	Epidemic.
1525	Resistance to 'Amicable Grant', particularly in East Anglia.
1526	Debasement of coinage.
1529	*Meeting of the Reformation Parliament.*
1536	The Pilgrimage of Grace. Mainly religious and political in character, but some social grievances also voiced.

CHAPTER 1

The population of England

The economic development of England between the mid fourteenth and the early sixteenth century was determined by changes in the country's population more than by any other single factor. This is undoubted, but unfortunately for historians these changes cannot be measured precisely. Three problems, in particular, confront us, the extent of the fall in England's population caused by the Black Death and by subsequent epidemics, the chronology of decline and recovery, and the possible redistribution of population throughout the country. The third question is so closely related to changes in the forms of rural settlement and to the growth and decline of towns that it is best considered in these contexts; the present chapter will concentrate on the scale of mortality and the fluctuations in the total population of England in the century and a half before 1529.

The historian's main difficulty in examining these problems is that medieval man was not statistically minded, and that consequently precise data are not available to us in our search for answers to problems. It is easier to judge the impression which the Black Death made on men's minds, for this is reflected in the chroniclers' writings, than to measure the scale of its ravages. The St Albans writer Thomas Walsingham declared that scarcely two men survived out of twenty in certain religious houses, and that many men considered that barely a tenth of the whole population remained alive (32, i, 273). Other chroniclers, such as Henry Knighton at Leicester, describe the extent of the plague locally, suggesting that there were 700 deaths in one parish and 380 in another, and some even appear to have doubted if man's life on earth was going to continue (53, p.169). Some figures of deaths in monastic houses may be accurate, but as the plague did not strike evenly throughout the country it would be foolish to deduce any estimate of national mortality from them. The same problem of interpretation arises from any use of manorial records, probably the best available documentary source; these can tell us no more than the number of holdings which fell vacant on particular estates and throw no light on mortality among landless persons.

The Black Death, which reached England in 1348, remained virulent in the following year, and recurred frequently in succeeding centuries, probably originated in central Asia and spread to the Black Sea area along the trans-Asian trade routes. From there it travelled rapidly to the Middle East, Italy and western Europe. The plague took two forms, bubonic, transmitted by a bacterium carried by the rat flea, and pneumonic, spread directly by droplet infection in a manner similar to the common cold. It is almost certain that both forms of the disease were present in late-fourteenth-century England, and it may well have been the pneumonic form, the more lethal of the two, which was responsible for the scale of the mortality in 1348–49 (53, pp.172–3). There has been some controversy in

9

recent years over the effect which the plague had on the population, and the bacteriologist J. F. D. Shrewsbury has tried to argue that bubonic plague could not, by its nature, have destroyed as high a proportion of the population as historians have claimed (102). He does not, however, allow for the possible effects of the pneumonic form of the disease, and suggests that another epidemic, possibly of typhus, may have been responsible. As far as the effects of population change on the economy are concerned, however, the particular disease is of secondary importance.

The greatest problem for the historian of late medieval population in England is that he has no reliable figure for the number of inhabitants at the time when the plague struck the country first. Indeed, since the Domesday Survey of 1086 there had been no government measure which had produced a record of this. A generation after the first onset of the disease, the poll-tax levy of 1377 did provide such figures, but it is clearly impossible to use this to estimate the level of population before 1348 or indeed the scale of mortality in the first, or any of the intervening later, epidemics. Furthermore, although the first poll-tax was sufficiently successful as a fiscal measure for it to be repeated in 1379 and 1381, the hostility shown to it in the Great Revolt of the latter year led to its abandonment as a form of taxation; not until the sixteenth century do further governmental records become available which can be employed to estimate the size of the national population with even a modicum of confidence. These include the returns of a military survey in 1522, the subsidy rolls of 1524–25 and the chantry certificates of 1545, which report the number of communicants in each parish. In other words, in the period covered by this book, the only direct evidence on population figures comes near its start and very close to, or even after, its end. There is literally nothing of an official nature which can serve as a guide to possible fluctuations in the intervening years.

Not only is the evidence scarce, but it is often undependable. The poll-tax was payable by all over the age of fourteen, apart from genuine beggars, including the mendicant friars, who were exempted from it, and from the inhabitants of Durham and Cheshire. The historian must therefore try to estimate the population of these two shires, the proportion of the population under fourteen and, hardest of all, the extent to which the tax was successfully evaded. Certainly evasion was rife in 1381, as can be seen from the marked discrepancies between the numbers paying the tax in that year and the figures for 1377 [A.4], and there is no reason to believe that the payments in the earlier year, although more complete, provide anything close to a total record of the population. Tax evasion is a similar problem in interpreting the sixteenth-century subsidy rolls, while any deductions based on the military survey, a crude census of males over the age of sixteen, must allow not only for children but also for the balance between men and women in the population as a whole. The chantry certificates of 1545, even if one accepts their record of communicants in the parishes as accurate, do not cover the whole country, and again there is uncertainty as to the proportion of the population below communicant age.

All estimates of population size must therefore allow for a large measure of conjecture, a fact stressed by all reputable modern historians who have worked on this intractable subject. The starting-point for all later studies must be J. C. Russell's survey of British medieval population, published in 1948 (99), but more recent work has been effectively synthesized in the extended paper by J. Hatcher, dating from 1977, which also provides an excellent bibliography (75). Russell estimated the population of England at just over 2¼ million in 1377, and suggested that it rose by nearly a million between then and 1545. Hatcher, by contrast, prefers a 1377 figure in the 2¾–3 million range, and thinks it unlikely that this was exceeded until the second quarter of the sixteenth century. If there was an increase by 1545, much of it may have come in the years after 1530, and become important economically only after the period covered by this book (75, p.69). What is even harder for historians to estimate is the extent of the fall in population before 1377 from its peak in the earlier years of the century, whether or not this point was reached around 1300, the most generally accepted date, or on the eve of the cataclysm caused by the Black Death.

In any attempt to estimate the effects which population changes could have on the economy as a whole, the crucial matter is, however, not the absolute numbers of Englishmen at any particular date but the broader demographic trend. Did the population remain more or less static after the dramatic decline in the second half of the fourteenth century, or did it make a rapid recovery from the first wave of epidemics? Here the problem is less difficult than the estimation of absolute figures, because further kinds of evidence can be employed in the search for an answer. In certain social groups it is possible to examine replacement rates, namely the number of children in a family who survived to adulthood. Two such groups, which are sufficiently well documented for such a study, are tenants-in-chief and the London alderman class. Work on the former group has shown that in the century between 1341 and 1440, and more markedly in the last three-quarters of this period, the replacement rate for males was clearly below one, but rose sharply by the turn of the fifteenth and sixteenth centuries (75, p.27). In the latter group the picture was very similar, a replacement rate of one in the generation following the Black Death, below one in the sixty years before 1437, and rising above it between then and the end of the century (104, p.204). Although both these samples suggest that there was a decline until well into the fifteenth century, followed by a recovery, there are two further points which need to be taken into consideration. Firstly, figures based upon the evidence of wills, which are the main source used in the examination of the London alderman class, may exaggerate the survival rate, because in times of plague whole families might be eliminated before any will could be drawn up, or between its drafting and the death of the testator. If this were the case, the drop in population in the first half of the period could have been deeper and the subsequent recovery slower than existing replacement figures suggest. Secondly, the fortunes of tenants-in-chief or of London aldermen and their families are not necessarily the best guide to trends in the country as a whole. One may presume that the standard of living of both these groups was above the national average, and that this could have given them better resistance to disease than their poorer neighbours. In the case of the Londoners, however, they may have been more vulnerable to plague than were country dwellers, unless they themselves had, as they might, country properties to which they could flee in time of pestilence. It seems clear that epidemics of the bubonic type became increasingly limited to the towns, which provided a better habitat for the plague-carrying black rat.

Attempts to examine survival and replacement rates in rural society and in towns other than London have made it clear that conclusions can at best be tentative. There are hints that in the country there was a higher survival rate from about the 1470s, but in Bristol and Worcester it appears that there was no marked population increase until about 1510 (59; 75, pp.28–9). If this is correct, and it is impossible to be certain how far the places for which adequate data survive are typical, it may indicate that rural areas saw an earlier recovery of population than the towns and certainly suggests that there were marked variations between different regions of the country.

Indirect evidence may also help the historian to examine population variations, because it is reasonable to infer that these caused economic changes, some of which can be measured over wider and more representative areas. The main problem associated with this approach is the difficulty of judging how far a rise or fall in the number of inhabitants was the vital factor in bringing about those changes of which we can be certain, notably those in wage and price levels. An alternative explanation for price rises, for example, has been to relate them to the amount of money in circulation or the bullion value of the coinage. This may have some validity; after the devaluation of the coinage in 1465, when its silver content was cut by 20 per cent, there was a price rise of 7 per cent. The total supply of money in circulation cannot, however, be measured, because although the value of coins struck is known for individual years, there is no satisfactory way of estimating how long they remained in circulation. The increase in wages, however, seems to have persisted even in periods when there was a dearth of money, and Hatcher is prepared to accept the general line of the arguments put forward in Postan's pioneering article of 1950 that population decline was the greatest single factor in bringing about these economic changes (75, pp.47–54).

The first indirect evidence for a falling population is the movement of wage-rates. Between 1300 and 1479 payments to agricultural workers on the estates of the bishops of Winchester rose sharply, both in cash terms and in real value, measured by the price of wheat. Furthermore, the wages of artisans, although they moved at a different rate, followed the same general pattern of increasing real values at approximately the same dates. There was, moreover, a decline in wage differentials between craftsmen and unskilled workers, a development which regularly occurs when labour is scarce and higher rates have to be paid, even to the unskilled. The substantial rise in the real value of wages in the late fourteenth century and for much of the fifteenth almost certainly reflects a shortage of workers. Since Postan wrote in 1950, the figures on which historians can base their opinions have been made conveniently available with the compilation of the Phelps Brown and Hopkins indices of the cost of consumable goods, and of building wage-rates in southern England, expressed in terms of these goods [A.1]. Obviously the tables must be used with caution; one lacks information of how far the figures for southern England, for both wages and prices, can be paralleled elsewhere in the country; also some short-term price fluctuations clearly reflect an individual harvest rather than any long-term population change. It is also clear that the prices of different commodities rose at varying rates and at different times. In the early sixteenth century the prices of essential goods rose more sharply than those of inessentials, and at the same time wage differentials increased again, so it is likely that by this date population was rising again, and that as real wages declined a higher proportion of them was being spent on essential goods and less on luxuries.

A second economic indication of declining population is the fall of land values from the mid fourteenth century. Payments for leases of demesne lands, which were freely negotiated and not protected by custom, provide the clearest picture of conditions. These were already declining by 1400 and apparently continued to do so throughout the fifteenth century. Where annual rents were protected by custom, the only payment which could be varied was the entry fine payable by a new tenant, and one can see a decline in these comparable with those in payments for leases. Shortly before the plague, entry fines on the Glastonbury estates were high, at the level of £12 a virgate, but a century later they were nominal. Instead of land being in demand, lords were having to accept tenants where they could find them, on conditions which the tenants were prepared to offer. Admittedly, there were regional variations in land values, and when they began to rise again, the increase was more marked in areas round London, where the demands for food from a large urban area pushed up the value of agricultural land. At the time when rent levels were falling, some less profitable land also went out of cultivation (although the extent of this is hard to measure), so it is clear that the fall in rents must have been due to a shortage of potential tenants rather than to a greater supply of land, which might have resulted from the clearance of forest or the reclamation of fenland.

Economic evidence, then, confirms the more direct pointers to population changes such as the study of replacement rates. There was a fall during the later decades of the fourteenth century and some recovery towards the end of our period. How far can one measure the chronology of these changes or plot rises and falls within it? This is difficult, particularly as most studies of the effects of the plague have tended to concentrate on the fourteenth-century epidemics, the Black Death of 1348–49 and the further outbreaks of the next generation, rather than on the recurrent visitations of the fifteenth century (*see* Framework). Perhaps the most striking point to note at the outset is that the Black Death itself had a comparatively limited effect on wages and the supply of land. Despite the extent of mortality in the first onset of the plague (and the evidence of heriot payments on the Winchester manors shows a death-rate there of at least 50 per cent), wages did not increase startlingly, and until about 1370 there was a rise in rents which corresponded with that in prices (60). This may suggest that the Statute of Labourers, passed in 1351 to curb wage demands, had some success for a number of years. A change came in the second half of the 1370s, when there was a sharp drop in prices at a time when wages continued to rise, and from 1377 until the middle of the 1390s the Phelps Brown index shows a markedly higher level of real wages. A possible explanation for this apparently delayed effect of the Black Death is that the first onset, despite its virulence, did not harm the economy as a whole as much as might have been expected, and that it was the continuing effect of later outbreaks which did the greater damage. There seems to be little doubt that before 1348 the country was overpopulated in relation to its resources – Hatcher estimates the pre-plague population in the 4½–6 million range, and probably nearer the higher figure (75, p.68) – and that the contribution which the extra population made to its total productivity was negligible. As a result, to quote Bridbury, the 'mid-century pestilences were more purgative than toxic' (60). If this were the case, why was there a change in the 1370s? It is possible that the earlier epidemics absorbed the existing population surplus and that the later outbreaks upset the balance between land and labour which had been re-established after 1350. It is perhaps noteworthy that two chroniclers refer to the plague of 1361 as the *pestis puerorum*, the plague of the children, and if it is true that children in particular had perished in that outbreak, it could be that by the early 1370s the supply of labour was being reduced by a shortage of new recruits, particularly as the survivors of 1361 would also have been attacked by another outbreak in 1369. The fall in population did not, however, mean a general decline in economic activity; rising wages may have served to increase consumption and give some stimulus to production, and it is worth noting that even the magnate class, which was more likely to suffer from the changed balance of power between land and labour through declining rent rolls and higher payments of wages was still able to invest considerable sums in new building during Richard II's reign.

As we move on to the fifteenth century, it is hard to judge the extent or the severity of individual outbreaks of plague or of other diseases, but it is probable that some of the epidemics which occurred in urban centres, where plague was most common, were on a sufficient scale to outweigh any natural increase in the population. In 1485 an epidemic, probably of the 'sweating sickness', carried away two mayors of London, and in the North at Ripon two mayors and six aldermen died in eight days, while York was also affected. It would be surprising if less prosperous sections of the community had not been equally attacked by disease at this time, and casualties of that extent would certainly have set back any recovery of the population. As late as the 1520s, a quarter of the property in Coventry was vacant and the population was substantially lower than in 1434, and the experience of other towns showed that this was not unique (75, p.65). The persistence of plague may have been partly responsible – the fact that the late summer remained a period of high mortality in an average year is compatible with the seasonal character of the disease (99, pp.196–8). It is probable that plague remained a constant threat, even if it is less well recorded in contemporary writings than at an earlier date; probably men were more inured to its presence than they had been in the first shock of 1348.

Population decline, of course, was not the only factor which could affect wages. Indeed, a series of bad harvests in the 1350s and 1360s, which increased food prices, may have been partly responsible for deferring the increase in real wages following the Black Death. Certainly it is noteworthy that it was 1377, a year of good harvest, which marked the start of the period when real wages remained high. Similarly, bad harvests probably explain the high prices and the

14

sudden fall in real wages in 1482 and 1483. In this context it is worth remembering that the late Middle Ages was a period of climatic deterioration, with lower temperatures and higher rainfull than in the thirteenth century and earlier. The results of this included some abandonment of cultivation in areas such as Dartmoor,where high contour settlements seem to have been effectively deserted by 1350, and problems in farming on heavy soils which could suffer from waterlogging. However, while climatic conditions could lead to some long-term changes in the economy and to sharp annual variations in food prices, there is no reason to doubt that over a long period movements in prices and wages do indicate whether population was rising or falling.

There has.been wide disagreement among historians concerning the chronology of population recovery, some suggesting that it started before the end of the fourteenth century, others favouring dates around 1430 and others again preferring the early sixteenth century (59; 75, p.15; 99, p.269). These disagreements themselves make it clear that there can have been no dramatic recovery which compensated for the losses from the fourteenth-century plagues; any such marked increase would have left no scope for argument. One must also stress that there is an insidious tendency to assume that once the population figures had reached their lowest point, their subsequent recovery was continuous; surviving evidence, however, suggests the contrary: that periods of rising population were at best intermittent and liable to sudden check from new epidemics. Whatever may have occurred earlier, it seems most likely that the sustained recovery of population did not take place until the late fifteenth or the early sixteenth century.

This conclusion would be supported by the evidence of the Phelps Brown index of real wages. The figures in this series are complete for the period covered by this book apart from a short gap between 1403 and 1411. They show considerable fluctuations in the annual level of real wages, but are markedly higher in the early fifteenth century than they had been in the late fourteenth. In some years in the 1430s wages failed to keep pace with high prices, but they rose again in the next two decades. After a slight decline in the 1460s, real wages again increased in the 1470s following a fall in prices, and the peak for the whole period of this book was reached in 1477. The 1480s show an average comparable with the 1430s, although this figure is probably depressed by the bad years of 1482 and 1483 – in the latter year prices were higher than they had been for a century, and wages did not rise proportionately. The two decades on either side of 1500 were comparatively stable, with wages being only a little lower than in the middle of the fifteenth century, but by the second decade of the sixteenth they began to decline in face of increasing prices. This decline continued, and in the 1520s wage-earners had less purchasing power than at any time since the 1370s [A.1].

Clearly, one cannot take price movements in southern England as a precise indication of population change even there, let alone over the country as a whole, but it would be extraordinary if variations in population were not an important factor affecting them, even taking into account the vagaries of individual harvests. It is possible that there may have been a recovery of population around 1430, as the previous decade was relatively free of plague, but from 1433 to 1454 epidemics again increased in frequency (*see* Framework), some being general throughout

the country and others being more localized, particularly in London. This was
followed by a lull of a decade before another series of major outbreaks between
1464 and 1479. This pattern of epidemics may explain the broad movement of
wages in the mid fifteenth century, for the 1440s, 1450s and 1470s, when it is
logical to assume that deaths were more likely to have exceeded births, were
precisely those decades when wages were highest.

When prices began to rise after 1480, the sharpest increases occurred in consumable goods, such as wheat, rather than in industrial products. This divergence
would be most easily explained by a rising population and a consequent labour
shortage. As wages declined, less money was available for purchasing inessential
goods, so the prices of these would rise less steeply. A further indication of
renewed population pressure is that complaints about land enclosure became
more conspicuous in the second decade of the sixteenth century, at precisely the
same time as real wages began to fall.

For studying the economy it matters little whether the population of England
in the 1520s had recovered to the level it had reached before the Black Death.
Hatcher, the most recent writer to survey the problem, suggests that it had come
nowhere near it (75, p.69). What is far more important is that the balance
between land and labour, which had been favourable to labour for about a century and a half, was now tilting back decisively in favour of the landowner.
Although there were various epidemics ahead, of various kinds, these no longer
prevented the population from entering on a period of sustained growth between
1525 and 1550.

In conclusion, the population of England remained fairly stable for much of
the fifteenth century, at a far lower level than in the first half of the fourteenth.
There may have been intermittent recoveries, but the bulk of the evidence (often
intractable and indirect) suggests that until around 1500 they were only temporary. This stability, not to say stagnation, underlies the whole economic condition
of late medieval England. The main beneficiary of it was the agricultural worker
and the principal loser the landowner. But the towns were by no means insulated
from its far-reaching effects, nor, within the towns, the trading community which
made a substantial contribution to the wealth of the kingdom in this period. How
each of these groups was affected will be considered in the chapters which follow.

CHAPTER 2

The rural economy and standards of living

The majority of the inhabitants of late medieval England lived close to the soil and were engaged in agriculture. There were, of course, regional variations in the form of agriculture pursued, and in some parts of the country the economy was more diversified. Throughout our period, for example, tin-mining provided alternative employment in parts of Cornwall, and the demand for food by those engaged in this occupation provided a stimulus to local agriculture. The development of textile manufacturing in the fifteenth century was not only one of the most fundamental economic changes of the period, but it also took men away from farming, created a market for the sale of agricultural products and gave an incentive to the producer to grow crops and raise stock beyond the levels required for his own consumption. The development of farming beyond the subsistence level was most marked in areas of urbanization. In South-east England, for example, the demand of London for food supplies affected the neighbouring counties and gave opportunities to enterprising farmers and traders. It also tended to increase the cost of land more markedly in this region than elsewhere.

Besides the varying effects caused by such economic factors as supply and demand, the basic soil conditions of particular areas provided more fundamental reasons for a range of types of farming. Even within a single county there could be marked differences in the capacity of the soil to yield particular crops, and in ease of cultivability. Joan Thirsk's brilliant examination of these variations, region by region, illustrates this for the period from 1500 onwards (103, pp.1–112), and there is no reason to believe that a similar diversity did not exist at the earlier period also, although there were probably changes in detail in particular areas, such as those caused by climatic change to which allusion was made in Chapter 1. Also, during the fifteenth century there was a more considerable transforming influence in the movement for enclosures, which had brought an increasing area under grazing at the expense of arable (Ch.5). Most recent historical work on the rural economy has involved studies in depth of particular regions or even individual manors, and despite the patchiness of the surviving evidence it is clear that one cannot draw hard and fast lines of distinction between regions of arable farming and those of stock-rearing. Certainly, there were broad differences between areas where the plough was dominant and those where grassland was typical, but within these areas there were many deviations from the norm.

If it is hard to generalize about the pattern of farming, it is no easier to summarize the resources or standing of the men who worked on the land. The term 'peasant' is a convenient abstraction, but no more, and there was no such person as a typical peasant. Some were of servile status and others free, although with the passage of time more and more secured their freedom (Ch.4), some might occupy barely enough land to sustain themselves and their families, while others accumulated substantial farms and became themselves employers of labour. The most important common feature among them was that they did not have absolute rights over the land which they farmed, but that they were in some way dependent on a lord, who had a right to some part of their labour or their profits from the land. One must remember that in different contexts the question, 'Whose land is this?' could be answered, equally correctly, by giving the name of the lord, the peasant or possibly that of some intermediate tenant.

The availability of land played a crucial part in relations between the land-owning class and those immediately concerned with its cultivation. Before the epidemics of the mid fourteenth century a serious land shortage existed, and the landowners had the opportunity to secure high rents for lands which they leased out, and to pay low wages to men lacking other opportunities for livelihood. Because labour was cheap, there were ample advantages in cultivating the demesne, and, because land was scarce, the lord had the whip-hand also if he wished a cash rent in lieu of labour services. Surprisingly, the widespread mortality of the plague of 1349 did not completely upset the balance of power between lord and peasant. It created some problems, which prompted the issue of the Ordinance of Labourers of 1349 and the later statute of 1351, which attempted to limit mobility of labour and to peg wage-rates at the 1346 level. These measures probably had a foundation in genuine agricultural unrest – the court rolls of St Albans Abbey record an increase in the number of fugitive villeins in the 1350s – but in most places the records suggest that survivors of the epidemic took up vacant holdings, at least those on land of reasonable quality, so it appears that the population surplus from the period before the Black Death still sufficed to provide a reservoir of possible tenants. Either through this, or through their exercise of coercive powers, the great landed nobility were able to minimize damage to their incomes in the first twenty years or so after the first onset of the plague.

It was in the 1370s that the balance of the economy was seriously altered; from 1372 there was a fall in basic food prices but no drop in wages, and this continued for some years, putting pressure on the profit margins which the manorial lords could secure from their estates (60). It is not clear whether the immediate cause of this was a fortuitous series of better harvests or a further decline in population following later outbreaks of plague. The results of the changed balance are more certain; there were attempts at repressing wages by law, and this may have contributed to the outbreak of the Great Revolt of 1381 (Ch.3). The lords' position was still fundamentally weak, and the shortage of labour in relation to land was now the main characteristic of the English rural economy. This was to lead to an increase in real wages and to a decline in rents for land, and in so far as these can be used to measure the standard of living of the people, they suggest that the condition of the peasantry improved markedly in the fifteenth century. It also undermined the economic resources of the landowners, although here one must stress considerable regional variations – the land market in South-east England remained buoyant because of its proximity to the London market, which provided an outlet for agricultural produce. The complementary nature of the urban and rural economies did not, however, prevent tensions between town and country, as in 1471 when discontent in Essex at the low prices paid for food by the Londoners led men from the county to join the attack on London by the Lancastrian leader Fauconberg (40, p.218).

The shortage of labour forced the landowners to change their methods of exploiting their estates, most obviously in the abandonment of direct cultivation of the demesne by the lord's paid men in favour of leasing it out for a cash rent. Precisely when this occurred can seldom be determined on any estates, because there are few series of complete manorial records, but it is safe to say that by the early fifteenth century the change had taken place widely on both lay and ecclesiastical lands, the latter being better documented over different parts of the country. This indeed was one of the most marked steps in the transition from the traditional medieval economy to the modern.

Of the lands in lay hands, the two crown duchies of Cornwall and Lancaster possess some of the fullest records, although they are by no means unique. The Cornish lands, however, do not fit into the normal pattern of tenures, for demesne exploitation there had been abandoned before 1300, if indeed it had ever existed (76, pp.10–11). In the Norfolk manor of Forncett the policy of leasing the demesne was adopted between 1358 and 1373, but on some of the Percy lands the practice did not appear till later. Although Cockermouth was leased as early as the thirteenth century, the family's five Yorkshire manors were still in demesne in 1352, three of these being leased by 1405 and all by 1416, while their four Sussex manors were all leased between 1405 and 1416.

A similar tendency can be seen on ecclesiastical estates. On those of the archbishop of Canterbury, leasing began in the 1380s and 1390s, and despite occasional returns to direct exploitation, by 1440 all the demesne fields had been leased. The abbey of Leicester came to depend increasingly on rent income from its demesnes, and also from its tithes, and most demesnes were rented by 1477, while Owston Abbey in the same shire had abandoned direct exploitation of demesne lands in all but three villages before 1400. In the North, at Durham Priory, some leasing of demesne began in the late fourteenth century, but the main period at which it was rented out was between 1408 and 1416, perhaps some two decades later than at Christ Church, Canterbury (80, pp.79, 90, 131; 209 p.272).

How far did the abandonment of demesne lands affect the income of the landowners? Certainly when the population was declining, one would expect that tenants might be hard to find and that concessions to them might be necessary, either in the form of a rent reduction or a cut in the entry fine, or in an extension of the period of the lease. Surviving evidence suggests that this was the case, although there were many local fluctuations. On the Talbot estate of Whitchurch in North Shropshire entry fines were lower in the early fifteenth century than in the late fourteenth, and there was a decline in the rents paid for demesne lands after 1400, and little sign of recovery until well into the sixteenth century. Court profits (which included entry fines) fell before 1400 and remained depressed as late as 1507, and the revenues from mills and tolls, already declining in 1400, also showed no recovery by the early sixteenth century. On the Leicester Abbey estates, of which 75–80 per cent fell within the shire, rent income in 1408 was nearly a fifth lower than in 1341, and by 1477 had fallen by almost a third on the 1341 figure, despite the fact that the proportion of income obtained from rent as opposed to production had risen. At Forncett, the average rent per acre of lands leased was markedly lower in the fifteenth century than in the late fourteenth, although one cannot tell from the published figures how far the fluctuations may have been due to variations in the quality of the particular pieces of land being leased at the time rather than to a general decline in rent levels. On the Canterbury estates, the initial period of leasing from 1380 to 1440 was followed by a time when it was harder to secure tenants, but after about 1490 there was some recovery in revenues and evidence that there was competition for leases (80, pp.79, 86).

Further instances could be multiplied, but would add little to the general picture. More important are some of the problems implicit in it. There is little doubt that it was the labour shortage which caused the shift to leasing, but although this provided more revenue than persistence in demesne farming would have done it still left the landowner with reduced resources. Despite this, one still sees lay lords investing in land – there was no possible alternative – and the need to compensate for declining returns to maintain an existing standard of living may indeed explain some of the characteristic features of fifteenth-century society, the pursuit of heiresses, the search for the patronage of a greater man, particularly the King who could grant pensions and offices, and the desire to campaign overseas. If even attempts to improve the standard of estate management did not raise the level of the returns (and the study of the Talbot Whitchurch estates suggests that these were more affected by the underlying economic conditions than by the standard of management), the only prospect for a lord was to seek some supplementary income beyond that of his estates. The one lay lord whose scope was seriously limited in this was of course the greatest, the King, who could seek no patron, and whose fiscal resources from taxation had to be charged on men whose own landed resources were under pressure.

Ecclesiastical landowners were also at a disadvantage compared with laymen. Their own acquisitions of property were severely curtailed by the provisions of the Statute of Mortmain of 1279, and they could not seek heiresses, offices or the profits of war. But they too had expenses, notably the cost of maintaining their buildings, and if voluntary gifts were insufficient to meet requirements, they might well run into difficulties. It is more remarkable that the religious houses survived so well than that they were faced with economic problems, and if they were sometimes regarded as grasping landlords, they had little option to be anything else. Nor was it only their tenants who were resentful, but they also had to face envious glances at their lands from the laity, some of whom at any rate seem to have considered them suitable prey. A scheme of disendowment was voiced in 1395, probably by Lollard sympathizers, though it did not reach Parliament, and in 1404 and 1410 proposals were put forward in Parliament for appropriating the temporalities of the clergy. Although none of these were put into effect, they illustrate the vulnerability of clerical resources in men's minds, and the potential danger to them if the Church did not have powerful support. In practice, however, the Church lost little – the suppression of the 'alien priories' by Henry V merely saw the conversion of resources to other ecclesiastical establishments, and the disappearance of a small number of decayed religious houses in the late fifteenth and early sixteenth centuries was caused by the transfer of their endowments to other houses or to colleges at universities (218, ii, 163–5, iii, 157–8).

When lands were leased out, a wide range of people took them up. In some cases groups of villagers rented them, in others local landowners and in others again merchants, who took them on a speculative basis (209, p.282). If the tenant could not exploit the land directly himself, with his own resources and those of his family, he would have to hire labour, but it seems likely that the small farmer was able to make a better profit than the great man, because his lands were not encumbered by a costly and unproductive bureaucracy. At Durham Priory, for example, less than half of the income assigned to each office in the monastery was devoted to the activity for which the office had been created; the rest was absorbed in management costs (209, p.255).

It is in peasant society that one sees some of the main gainers from the surplus of land. It is clear that there was considerable freedom in the peasant land-market, so that individuals were able to buy parcels of land and increase their own holdings. Such peasant land purchases reflect the recognition of their rights in the land, subject to the fulfilment of obligation to their lords. Again one can see local variations: in Kent, where there was partible inheritance by the local custom called gavelkind, peasant holdings were subject to constant division and could then be reconsolidated, because the holders of land had a free right to alienate it. Even in a single shire one can see adjacent villages where there were differences. In Leicestershire, the communities at Wigston and Ulston were largely free, whereas Foston, only 2 or 3 miles from Wigston, and Galby were occupied largely by servile tenants (83, pp.53–4). It was presumably where the community was predominantly free that one finds continual buying and selling of land between peasant families and the consequent development of a group of more prosperous men in the community. Of course, differences in wealth between peasant families were not new; the evidence of the poll tax returns shows that by the last quarter of the fourteenth century peasants might employ labour on their own account and even have a servant living in their household, although it is difficult to say how common this was (81, pp.30–3; 83, p.31). Such wealthier peasants could easily become dominant figures in a village, because surprisingly few communities had a resident lord. The poll tax returns for some areas in the West Midlands suggest that little more than one village in ten had resident gentry, and in Leicestershire the situation seems to have been similar, and to have remained so into the sixteenth century. By 1525 in the latter shire a quarter of the personal estate in a sample of forty villages was owned by 4 per cent of the rural population, excluding the squires – clearly there were some members of the peasantry who must have had sufficient wealth to dominate their fellows (81, pp.26–7; 83, pp.17, 142).

The purchase of land also presupposes that the peasantry involved were able to accumulate cash, which can have been done only by the production of surplus crops and their sale in a market. In some cases the purchasers of land came from outside the village, as at Leighton Buzzard in Buckinghamshire, where recent arrivals in the manor were able to build up their holdings. Men might also leave the land, members of Wigston families migrated to Leicester into commerce, and it reflects the mobility of the population that only about 10 per cent of the families there survived in the male line from 1377 to the time of Henry VIII. Some died out or moved away, others survived only in the female line and the lands passed to another family by marriage (81, pp.43–7; 83, p.31).

It is when one recognizes the variations in peasant advancement among even individuals in a single community, as well as from one village or one region to another, that one appreciates the need for caution in calling the fifteenth century the golden age of the English labourer. Although wage-rates and rent levels provide one measure of the peasant standard of living, there are dangers in reading too much into this. Firstly, such figures give only an average, and some men would therefore do far less well. Secondly, and far more important, the main factor in most men's standard of living was not what they could earn but what they could produce, and here conditions were dominated not by economic relationships with other men but by something far more basic, the annual and unpredictable variations in the weather and the effects which this would have on the harvest. In some cases this might be literally a matter of life and death. For what this might involve, the historian must rely on literary material, and Langland's dialogue, between Piers and Hunger in the B text of *Piers Plowman* rings painfully true as a description of peasant hardship in the pre-potato age.

Piers did not have meat, but only cheese, loaves of beans and bran and various vegetables, and it was on these that he would have to live until Lammas and the new harvest. He had a cow and a calf, so he presumably would have milk, which together with the cheese could supply some protein in his diet. Indeed, milk probably became more plentiful about May, the notional time of Langland's vision, although the continuation of the passage suggests that in other respects this was a bad time of year. When harvest came, the people could put Hunger to sleep. Langland is critical of some of their actions; Waster and the beggars scorned poor food and demanded better, fine bread instead of that with beans in it and well-cooked meat. Despite the element of social criticism in the poem, Langland takes a conservative attitude to popular discontent, criticizing demands for high wages and murmurs against the Statute of Labourers. The passage concludes with a prophecy of renewed famine and deaths from hunger.

One cannot say how accurate this picture is in detail, nor if Langland is describing a famine or normal peasant conditions. However, it certainly shows the importance of seasonal variations on the normal diet of the people, and particularly of the poor. The 'poor widow' of Chaucer's *Nun's Priest's Tale* had a diet consisting mainly of milk and brown bread, with broiled bacon and the occasional egg, and this may represent a fairly normal diet. Chaucer, writing for an aristocratic audience, would be less inclined to dwell on such incidental details or to consider seasonal variations than Langland, whose central theme at this point in the work was that of hunger. A chronicle source confirms Langland's remark about bread being made from materials other than grain, namely beans, peas and vetches, but it should be noted that this year, 1439, saw a great dearth of corn, and the chronicler's comment probably reflects the unusual nature of the food, at least in his eyes; we do not know how far this view would be general and how far it was that of a man whose conditions were normally more affluent. The year 1439 was in fact one of the worst periods of famine in the fifteenth century; it had followed a harvest failure, brought about by heavy rains over the whole country throughout the summer of 1438. Wheat prices at 13s. 4d. a quarter were more than double the normal (though not as disastrously high as in the notorious famine years of 1315–17), barley at 6s.–7s. was up by over 50 per cent and peas and beans at 6s. had tripled in cost (209, pp.266–7).

These were the main items of agricultural produce, although there were many variations in the quantity of each grown, presumably resulting from local soil conditions. At four dates between 1393 and 1470, peas and beans represented from 28 to 32½ per cent of the crops on the Leicester Abbey estates, barley (presumably mainly used for brewing) from 40 to 45 per cent and wheat from 11½ to 14½ per cent. The rest of the crops consisted of oats and rye. At Wigston (also Leicestershire) in the early sixteenth century peas and beans were even more important at 49¼ per cent, barley represented 43½ per cent and wheat only 6 per cent. There was a negligible quantity of rye (80, p.63; 83, p.156). The main problem of studying agricultural production is the lack of clear evidence on yields in relation to seed, although at Battle in Sussex, where this can be documented, wheat and barley yields seem to have declined and those of oats increased during the later Middle Ages. This may reflect developments elsewhere in England, as it seems to be part of a general European pattern of production.

In the mid fifteenth century Sir John Fortescue claimed that the English were richer than the French, that they normally drank ale instead of water and ate all kinds of flesh and fish in abundance (10, pp.86–7). Although his view is probably idealized and unlikely to be particularly informed about peasant conditions, there is some evidence to support his assertions. The accounts of an establishment of chantry priests at Bridport in Dorset show that their diet contained considerable quantities of flesh and fish, and that, although it normally was fairly plain, it could contain luxuries on special occasions. These priests may have been more affluent than the rest of the population, but one has evidence of flesh-eating in the artisan class too. During a heresy trial in 1429, a deposition against Margery Baxter, a wright's wife from Martham in Norfolk, stated that she had been seen boiling *unam peciam de Baken* on the Saturday after Ash Wednesday. She also said that it was better to eat left-over meat in Lent than go to market and incur debt through buying fish (241, p.128). In this remark, perhaps the earliest preserved utterance of an English housewife, she certainly seems to have assumed that such food would be a normal part of the family diet. It is likely, too, that among the peasantry occasional poaching might supplement the meat element in a family's food.

One major factor in causing seasonal variations in food supplies was the difficulty of storage. The wealthier classes might have stone-built barns, which could protect their supplies, but houses built of timber and mud, and with earth floors, would be very damp, so it would be hard to protect grains both from rotting and from the depredations of rats and mice. Building materials for peasant houses varied between different parts of the country. In the clay land areas, little stone was available for building, and timber remained the main material of houses, even as late as the fifteenth century. Excavations at two sites deserted at this period, Goltho in Lincolnshire and Barton Blount in Derbyshire, have shown this. In the West Midlands, the evidence of the Worcester court rolls suggests a prevalence of timber-framed buildings, most often consisting of three bays, although some were larger, and it is possible that the smaller houses were less well recorded. In some areas there were stone buildings, and the houses were partially paved, as at Barrow Mead in Somerset, deserted around 1400. In the last thirty years archaeological investigation of deserted village sites has added substantially to our knowledge of peasant conditions, and will probably provide more information in future, particularly by enabling fuller comparisons to be made between different parts of the country.

Such evidence, however, has its limitations. Until far more excavation has been completed, it will be hard to distinguish between what is typical of an area and what is unusual. Chronology of building forms can be established only approximately, and archaeology cannot tell us of variations in the prosperity of a community from one year to the next. As this is one of the main characteristics of the late medieval rural economy, one must not expect too much from the evidence of excavations. Documentary material, however sparse it may be, provides a firmer chronological framework for the historian.

CHAPTER 3

The Peasants' Revolt

In view of the hardships endured by many peasants, even at times when they were making some gains at the expense of their lords, it is hardly surprising that there were outbreaks of discontent, some of which took violent forms – indeed it has been said that peasant movements were as much a part of seigneurial society as strikes are of large-scale capitalism. One may pursue this parallel further, and suggest that, just as many strikes in modern industry are prompted by particular local conditions, and reflect immediate discontents rather than any general revolutionary outlook, equally many peasant movements had no wide aims, but merely indicate a grievance against a particular manorial lord.

At first sight the revolt of 1381 is different. It drew support from a wide area in South-east England, and there were associated outbreaks in other parts of the country, ranging from York and Scarborough in the North-east, to the Wirral in the North-west, and to Bridgwater and Ilchester in Somerset. It is the rising which has become known as 'the Peasants' Revolt' without any further qualification and has been seen as the most serious social revolt which occurred in medieval England. Yet despite its geographical spread, it is hard to find common features among the different risings which would justify the idea that the revolt was in any real sense a common movement. Undoubtedly the risings were connected with each other in so far as the news of the initial outbreak in Essex seems to have sparked off further unrest in adjacent counties, and later in more remote parts, and it is certain that the general circumstances of the time created an atmosphere which was ripe for revolt, but the differences of aim among the different groups of rebels suggest that each had its own grievances which it hoped to right by force. The various risings must be seen as spontaneous popular movements, and there is no reason to believe in any central leadership which attempted to control the revolt.

Indeed, the divergence in background among the different groups of rebels may reasonably raise the question whether the rising of 1381 is best described by its traditional name, whether it was in fact a peasants' revolt. The troubles at York and Scarborough, already mentioned, took place in an urban environment, and very conspicuous in the troubles was the city of London. Of the 287 participants in the rising who were excluded by name from the general amnesty, over half, 154, were Londoners (98, p.cxxiii; 109, p.55). It is clear, too, that although most of the Londoners involved were drawn from the poorer classes of society, matters were complicated by factions in the city government. An attempt was made to inculpate a group of five aldermen with participation in the troubles, but it is unlikely that in at least four cases there was any real foundation for the charge.

The revolt is well documented, both in chronicles and in the records of government.[1] Full though these are, they are not always very helpful – much of the chronicle material depends on hearsay, although the author of the *Anonimalle Chronicle* seems to have been an eye-witness of events in London or at least to have had access to some eye-witness account. A more serious problem is the bias of the sources, which reflect the views of the ruling class rather than those of the rebels and therefore tend to paint a picture of disorder rather than to record the grievances which prompted the revolt.[2] Such chronicles include letters which purport to have been written by the rebels, and note demands which were made during the rising. These, taken together with inferences drawn from what the rebels did, go some way to explaining why the revolt took place.

There is a substantial amount of evidence for peasant discontent before 1381, most of it (as far as existing evidence shows) being concentrated in the Central and East Midlands and in the Home Counties, precisely those parts of England where manorialization was most fully developed. However, there was a significant absence of such discontent in East Anglia and Kent, two of the areas most severely affected in 1381 (78, p.145). Disputes, both before and after 1381, were concerned with questions of rents to be paid and services to be performed, or with whether or not individuals were free men or villeins. Although some of the grievances voiced in 1381 concerned these same matters, there were other factors at work too, which may help to explain the special character of this rising.

The broad lines of the revolt are clear (11, pp.38–44) although there are numerous problems of detail. The first outbreak occurred in Essex in the second half of May, in the form of resistance to taxation, by early June Kent also was in revolt, and by the second week of that month East Anglia too was affected. In mid-June the Kent rebels marched on London, where they were joined by the Essex men and secured support from discontented elements in the capital. For some three days there was a virtual collapse of government, during which the rebels laid hands on and put to death the Chancellor, Archbishop Sudbury, and the Treasurer, Sir Robert Hales. The death of the rebel leader Wat Tyler on 15 June changed the situation, and by the following week the authorities were again in control in the South-east. The climax of the East Anglian revolt came slightly later; there was widespread trouble in Norfolk, Suffolk and Cambridgeshire between 12 and 21 June, in which the main victims were the Chief Justice of the King's Bench, Sir John Cavendish, and the prior of Bury St Edmunds. The man principally responsible for suppressing the trouble was Bishop Despenser of Norwich, whose force crushed various rebel groups between 18 and 25 or 26 June.

What were the causes of the rising? Were they predominantly political or social? Undoubtedly taxation provided the occasion for the revolt; this was stressed by the best informed contemporary source, the author of the *Anonimalle Chronicle*, and by the Leicester canon Henry Knighton (11, pp.124, 135). This was prompted by the costs of war – indeed, since the renewal of the conflict with France in 1369 there had been several major fiscal exactions, of which the three poll taxes were the last. In 1377 the tax had been levied at 4d. a head, in 1379 it had been graduated and in December 1380 Parliament granted a further tax at 1s. a head, and although suggestions were made that the rich should help the poor to meet this heavy burden, one suspects that these were largely unheeded. Even in 1377 there seems to have been considerable evasion; in 1381 this was certainly far worse. In those cases where the figures from counties and boroughs have survived from both 1377 and 1381, those for the latter year show an average fall of 32.54 per cent. As there is no natural reason for this, such as an epidemic, one must assume widespread evasion as the cause. In only one place, the borough of Northampton, was the 1381 figure higher than that for 1377; elsewhere it is down, sometimes by a very large amount [A.4].

The figures suggest two obvious conclusions, that the authority of the central government, as measured by its ability to secure payment, was weakest in the remote areas of the North and West, and that on the whole it was easier to enforce payments in the boroughs than in the countryside. No borough showed a drop of over 50 per cent in the numbers paying and only four over 45 per cent, whereas two counties showed one of over 60 per cent, four more of between 50 and 60 per cent and one more of over 45 per cent. At the other end of the scale, only three counties showed a fall of under 15 per cent, while nine boroughs (excluding Northampton) come into this group. Apart from these conclusions, there is little that can be safely deduced from these figures, as there is no obvious correlation between the areas of major disorder and particular levels of tax evasion. Possibly the markedly low figures for both Cambridgeshire and the town of Cambridge indicate effective enforcement of the tax, and in Kent, Norfolk and Suffolk, too, the figures are below average, although less conspicuously so, but in Essex and Hertfordshire they are higher.

The taxation in itself, however heavy, could hardly have sparked off so violent a conflagration if conditions had not been appropriate for it. One may eliminate famine as a possible underlying cause of discontent, as the harvests in the five years before 1381 were at least average and sometimes good (78, p.161). The demands made by the rebels provide the clearest guide to their grievances, and according to the *Anonimalle Chronicle* those put forward by the Essex men at Mile End on 14 June were that they should be allowed to seize and punish traitors, and that no man should be made a serf nor do homage or any type of service to a lord in return for land; instead they should hold it at a rent of 4d. an acre. This suggests that grievances were both political and social. Significantly, on the following day at Smithfield, after the deaths of Sudbury and Hales, there seem to have been no further demands concerning 'traitors', but further ones about social and legal status, that there should be no lordship apart from the King's, that the Church should be disendowed and (cryptically) that there should be no law except that of Winchester (11, pp.161–5). The other chroniclers are less explicit, but give a similar impression, complaints about servitude and oppression and demands for liberty bulking largely in their accounts. Knighton includes among the demands one for free rights of hunting and fishing, and Walsingham also reports an alleged confession by the rebel leader Jack Straw, which suggested far more revolutionary aims, the killing of all the lords and later of the King, the destruction of all possessioner clergy, leaving only the friars, and the creation of kings in all the counties (11, pp.180–6, 201–7, 365–6). This confession must be treated with scepticism, although it possibly has some factual substratum and is not merely a figment of Walsingham's imagination. The idea, however, that the rebels aimed to kill the King is unlikely – not only did the rebels show a positive loyalty to him at Mile End and Smithfield, and adopt as a watchword 'King Richard and the True Commons', but they made no attempt to take vengeance on him for the death of Wat Tyler, when he could have been at their mercy.

The actions of the rebels, as well as their demands, reflect both political and social aims. The hostility to alleged traitors took extreme form in the murders of Sudbury, Hales and Cavendish, and equally strong was the dislike of the King's uncle, John of Gaunt – his palace of the Savoy was burned down (although it is uncertain whether the Kentishmen or the Londoners played the leading part in this) and he would probably have shared the fate of Sudbury and the others if he had not had the good fortune to be in the North negotiating with the Scots. As it was, a number of the lesser victims of the rising were associates of Gaunt, and almost certainly owed their fate to his unpopularity. Other sufferers from popular hatred were foreigners, particularly Flemings, a number of whom were killed in London and East Anglia (78, pp.195–8). It is not clear if there were particular economic motives for these killings, or if they were simply a matter of xenophobia. Yet another target of the rebels' attack was lawyers and legal records. Here, particularly in the destruction of manorial court rolls, which provided a record of the obligations owed to the lords of the manors, one sees the desire to be free of the legal burdens which were laid on peasant tenants. The demand for personal freedom, a recurrent feature in late medieval peasant society, does not reflect only a wish for improved social status, but also a hope for potential economic advantages. As long as a man was unfree, he had no access to the royal courts, but could plead only in his lord's court. A free man, on the other hand, could appeal in the public courts against any increase in the burdens imposed on him. Furthermore, he could leave the manor if he so wished, and could therefore negotiate for better terms from the lord by threatening to go if the latter refused concessions (79, p.31). The most plausible explanation of the demand for the law of Winchester is probably that the rebels accepted the 1285 Statute of Winchester, which could be interpreted as giving all adult males the right to bear arms. Bearing arms and sharing in the maintenance of order, however, would give men additional powers.

Although the rebels' demands for personal freedom are conspicuous in the chronicles, this can hardly have been the main motive of the Kentishmen, one of the most prominent groups among the peasants, because in Kent there was no serfdom. Here perhaps the political factor was more significant. When Parliament met in the autumn of 1381, the Speaker expressed the view that the troubles had been caused by abuses in government, notably by purveyance for the royal household and by the levy of taxation for the defence of the realm, particularly as this did not prevent the King's enemies from raiding England. The *Anonimalle Chronicle* states that the Kentish rebels commanded those living within 12 leagues of the sea not to accompany the rebel army, but to stay at home to keep the coast free from enemies (11, pp.126–7, 330–1). As the south coast had been raided only a few years earlier, this action is understandable, and it also indicates a measure of political awareness among the peasant class. It would probably be dangerous to underestimate the amount of information which percolated down to the classes which were not themselves involved in government, and it is likely that echoes of the political crises of the 1370s, notably the events of the Good Parliament of 1376 (ch.16), were heard in the countryside. It is worth remembering that the London merchant Richard Lyons, who had been impeached in 1376, was one of the rebels' victims five years later.

It would be a mistake to assume that all participants in the revolt were involved in it for the same reasons. The rising created an atmosphere of disorder in which those with grievances felt free to take violent action against their enemies. This explains why one finds contrary demands being made by groups in different places. At Dunstable, where the rebels were townsmen, they tried to restrict freedom of trade to within the borough, whereas the rural Essex rebels had followed precisely the opposite policy, and at Yarmouth the insurgents, drawn from the neighbouring countryside attempted to overthrow the rights of the municipality (98, pp.41, 108–11).

There was little ideology in the revolt, although Christian teachings of social obligation played some part. These were voiced most clearly by the radical priest John Ball, whose record of inflammatory preaching had brought him into conflict with the authorities as early as 1366, and who had been imprisoned earlier in 1381 for his hostility to the Pope and the prelates (11, p.372). Many of his utterances were, however, sermon commonplaces, to which parallels can be found in other contemporary preaching. Even the famous couplet of Ball's sermon at Blackheath, as reported by Walsingham:

> When Adam dalf, and Eve span,
> Wo was thanne a gentilman?

was adapted from traditional preaching on the emptiness of human boasting. However, although it was not unusual for preachers to criticize social abuses and injustice, this was not necessarily given a revolutionary tone (230, pp.291, 296), and the significant point about Ball was that he adapted a traditional idea to revolutionary ends. It is also worth noting that after his death he seems to have remained as a hero in folk memory. Walsingham and Knighton also attempted to blame Wyclif and the Lollards for propagating revolt, but this must be seen only as scaremongering by the established order in the Church, attempting to tar the socially conservative academic heretic with the brush of revolution. Hilton's attempt to revive the idea of Lollard influence on the revolt by redefining Lollardy as something more than the following of Wyclif (78, p.213) disregards the general character of later Lollardy, which only rarely developed revolutionary tendencies.

Ball was the only prominent figure in the rising who had any known background of discontent; the other leaders emerged in the course of events. Even Wat Tyler, the most famous of these, does not seem to have been involved in the earliest disturbances in Kent, as he is not mentioned in indictments dealing with disorder in Canterbury on 10 and 11 June, when the leader was John Hales of Malling. Tyler is first mentioned (in conjunction with a John Rackstraw, presumably the man later known as Jack Straw) in a reference to a command issued on 13 June (11, pp.145–7). The uncertainty of even contemporary writers about who the leaders were, notably the fact that a number of them considered Straw and Tyler to be identical, illustrates how obscure they were. Attempts to trace the background even of Tyler have petered out through lack of definite evidence.

It is clear that in each area of revolt, some local figure emerged to take the lead, and this is hardly surprising when one considers the nature of fourteenth-century society. In each village and manor local men filled such offices as bailiff, and the holders of these positions were presumably the more articulate members of the community – inglorious the peasants may have been, but there is no need to regard this as synonymous with mute. Thomas Baker of Fobbing in Essex, whose resistance to the poll tax was the earliest recorded sign of revolt, had indeed been appointed to be village collector of the tax (11, p.205), but instead led the opposition to it. William Grindcob at St Albans and Geoffrey Litster in East Norfolk were local leaders as able and articulate as Tyler in Kent and London, and all seem to have had a capacity to maintain discipline. In Essex and Suffolk the rebels were sufficiently acquainted with the structure of local government to use the machinery of the hundreds for the purpose of mobilization (78, p.217). Some of the rebel leaders, notably Litster, may have appreciated their military weakness, because they attempted to involve members of the gentry in the revolt, and although they had little support of this nature, the very fact that they hoped to obtain it must argue against an interpretation of the revolt simply in class terms.

The spread of the revolt after the original outbreak reflects its improvised nature. Predictably, local risings were sporadic, but once the spark had been kindled, conditions were clearly ripe for revolt. It is hard, however, to see convincing evidence for the existence of any central revolutionary organization, and Hilton's demolition of the idea that there was something called the 'Great Society' is completely convincing (78, p.215). His translation of *magna societas* as 'large company' is far more probable, and it could refer to an individual rebel band which was threatening to dominate an area. No doubt there were communications between different groups, but the only ones preserved, those of John Ball (even if authentic), were cryptic allegorical utterances, not commands for action (11, pp.381–3; 78, p.214).

The rebels' attitude to the King is striking. Only Straw's 'confession' suggests hostility to him, and more characteristic was the attempt to identify Richard with their cause. However mistaken this attitude was, it undoubtedly was a significant factor in events (11, p.23: 78, p.225). It may explain both why the fourteen-year-old King played a prominent part in the negotiations at Mile End and Smithfield, and how he was able to avoid mob vengeance after Tyler's murder. It is not necessary to suppose that he acted on his own initiative, although this is implied in the *Anonimalle Chronicle* (11, pp.158–9): possibly his advisers felt that he might be less at risk than they themselves, and that in the circumstances a policy of temporary conciliation was the best course of action.

A problem deserving consideration is how strong the rebel forces actually were. Although all the contemporary writers depict widespread anarchy, it is hard to reconcile this with the speed of the government's reaction after Tyler's death. The mob undoubtedly was in control in London when Sudbury and Hales were executed, but on 15 June the civic leaders were able to raise a substantial force from the wards of the city and surround the rebel force at Smithfield, which immediately yielded. On this the sources are virtually unanimous (11, pp.167, 179, 186–7, 197, 204–11). If one remembers that the rebels had sympathizers in London, although these may have been partly alienated from them by the disorders, it is all the more remarkable how quickly the city authorities reasserted their control and obtained substantial support. Only one member of the feudal class, Sir Robert Knolles, is reported as playing a major part in the attack on the rebels in London, although the earl of Suffolk and Bishop Despenser of Norwich were prominent in the repression in East Anglia. Possibly the deaths of the Chancellor and the Treasurer undermined the confidence of the King's surviving ministers, and it was left to other loyalists to act on their own initiative.

The sudden collapse of the rising leaves one final question: did the revolt play any significant part in the development of English society in the following decades? The general view is that it was basic economic forces rather than the events of 1381 which brought about the end of villeinage and the enfranchisement of the peasant class (11, p.29). Alone among recent writers, Hilton suggests that the rising may have deterred the ruling class from further local attempts at repression (78, pp.231–2). One cannot judge which of these views is preferable, because one can only infer the motives of the landowners from their actions; we do not know if they were genuinely frightened by the memory of the revolt, or for how long any such fear persisted. Their treatment of those who held land from them may have been prompted as much by economic motives as by political or psychological ones. Certainly the suppression of the rising did not eliminate peasant unrest, although this reverted to being a purely local phenomenon, and in general to taking less violent forms. The most obvious casualty of the rising was the poll-tax, which was abandoned as a future source of revenue.

---

1. The main narratives and considerable documentary material are available in (11). Other documentary material is printed in the appendices to (98).
2. There is a valuable analysis of the sources in (11, pp.3–13).

CHAPTER 4

Rural society and popular movements after 1381

The rebellion of 1381 and its subsequent repression did not affect the underlying problems of the economy, notably those posed by the decline in population. The initial ruthlessness of the authorities was soon moderated, and pardons were granted to most of the participants in the rising, but sporadic disorder continued after 1381, although it was no longer a serious threat to society and government. During the fifteenth and early sixteenth centuries there were intermittent popular revolts, but apart from that of Jack Cade in 1450, they tended to be far more limited in scope than that of 1381. Also, although some of the demands which had been made in 1381 were echoed in the later risings, in none of them was there anything so clear-cut in the way of a social programme as the demands put forward at Mile End and Smithfield. Some popular attitudes did not change, and in London at any rate one sees recurrent attacks on foreigners and their property at times of civil or political commotion, as in 1456, 1457, 1463, 1470 and 1517. Such acts did not, however, amount to a programme of action; they merely represented instinctive hostility to outsiders. Although these troubles occurred in the city, foreigners were also attacked at times of peasant rioting when the rebels came to London, so it is clear that there were some sentiments which were shared by townsmen and countrymen alike.

Popular movements between the late fourteenth and the early sixteenth centuries are best understood in the broader context of developments in peasant society, even although most such risings seem to have been prompted by political or fiscal considerations rather than by social grievances. This does not, however, mean that the peasantry were contented, nor does it prove that they were particularly prosperous; rather it suggests that the peasantry found that they could secure their aims more effectively by passive resistance and the exploitation of their economic power than by violence. In Essex, a shire which had been at the heart of the 1381 troubles, the peasantry were able to improve their lot after the repression of the revolt. A statute of 1388 attempted to reinforce the Statute of Labourers, the measure enacted to control wages after the Black Death of 1348–49, but attempts in 1389 to put it into practice showed that men were trying to shake off the stigma of villein tenure, even at the cost of taking a cash wage worth less in real terms than the combination of cash and food which they had been paid previously, insisting on working by the day rather than contracting for a yearly wage, and exploiting the possibility of alternative employment (65, pp.92–5). Men who took such actions clearly felt that they had a secure prospect of work and that they did not need to be particularly submissive to their lords. The peasant's ultimate weapon was to leave the manor, and the example of Forncett in Norfolk shows that between 1400 and 1575, 126 serfs were recorded as

32

withdrawing to 64 different places. Over half did not go beyond 10 miles, and more than half of the remainder stayed within 20. One of the most popular destinations was Norwich, 12 miles away (65, pp.123–4). By going even so short a distance, however, men could free themselves from the control of their lord and the custom of the manor, and it is clear that one can see a similar situation elsewhere in the country; families were prepared to leave the land to free themselves from their lords (79, p.35).

Custom of the manor defined peasant obligations, but it could also help to determine peasant rights. There were different kinds of customary tenure, but they had in common the fact that they gave some protection to the unfree man against arbitrary expropriation. He was not protected by the King's court as a free man was, but most lords seem to have recognized that even unfree tenants had certain rights. The fifteenth century saw the development of what was called copyhold tenure, by which a peasant possessed a copy of the entry on the manorial court roll which defined his rights and obligations, as the most common form of land-holding in early modern England. This was not universal – some tenants held land by custom alone, without possessing a copy of the court roll entry, and they were generally more vulnerable to pressure from their lords, as legal protection was gradually extended to copyhold tenants by the courts both of common law and of equitable jurisdiction during the fifteenth century. In some areas, however, customary tenants seem to have been able to obtain security comparable to that enjoyed by copyholders. In so far as tenants were able to secure the protection of copyhold, it removed the old disadvantages under which the servile tenant laboured. By the end of the Middle Ages there were various categories of copyholder, the best placed being those who held by inheritance with the entry fine to the land being fixed, while the less fortunate held for a term of life, with an uncertain entry fine to be paid by the successor, or even, although this was unusual, held only for a term of years (79, p.47; 82, pp.60–2). One demand made during the Pilgrimage of Grace in 1536 was that entry fines should not exceed the value of two years' rent, so it is likely that by this time, when a rising population was creating a shortage of land, some landlords were seeking more. More vulnerable than copyhold tenants were leaseholders, particularly when their leases were granted for limited terms such as seven or ten years, with the possibility of the rent being raised at each renewal. This could be done, and the lord would be in a position to rack-rent, if there was any demand for land, and although this latter condition was not met for much of the fifteenth century, it did apply as the sixteenth century advanced. One must not, however, classify tenants too rigidly, because the same man might hold different parts of his lands by different forms of tenure, some freehold, some copyhold and some by lease. This indeed was a factor in hastening the decay of villeinage, because a man who was free would not wish to incur servile obligations if he took possession of land which had hitherto been burdened with them.

During the fifteenth century, the laws of supply and demand worked in favour of the peasantry. Population shortage had reduced the demand for land, and it was not until the sixteenth century that demand again began to exceed supply. Significantly, it was as the population recovered that one again sees widespread movements of social unrest. An example of the practical working of the economic balance of power can be seen on the estates of the bishopric of Worcester, where the peasants were able to nullify their lord's attempts at coercion by simply refusing to pay the sums demanded. This was reflected in the increasing arrears of payments owed between the episcopate of Bishop Wakefield in 1389 and that of Bishop Carpenter in 1454. Permanent arrears were normally written off at a bishop's death, so the figures give some indication of the rate at which they accumulated. In 1389, after fourteen years of Wakefield's episcopate they were £465, in 1412, after five of Peverell's they were £252, and in 1454, after ten of Carpenter's they were £1194, representing respectively an average annual increase in arrears of £33, £50 and £119. The Worcester accounts also show that the tenants' resistance was directed particularly at payments which testified to their servile status, such as tallage and payments to commute labour service. Behind these arrears is evidence of a collective refusal to pay, which the bishop's officers could not overcome. By the early sixteenth century, however, the figure of arrears dropped; as a rising population began to press on the means of subsistence, the lord had a more powerful weapon to hand. Servile obligations did survive, albeit unevenly, throughout the country, and their persistence in this way probably reflects the unevenness of the power struggle from one manor to another. It was probably because of the greater financial power which it offered them that the lords tried, where possible, to maintain servile obligations on their tenants (79, pp.48–55).

The relative absence of major revolts during the fifteenth century probably reflects the fundamental state of the economy, and it is perhaps a reasonable assumption that the basic prosperity of the peasantry in their relations with the land-owning class contributed to this. Some of the wealthier peasants undoubtedly prospered, rising in rank to become yeomen or even gentry in the sixteenth century, but these were a minority. The basic vulnerability of the peasantry was revealed when the economic climate became chillier, and for many families this period of prosperity was to prove short-lived. In the sixteenth century, rents and entry fines began to rise again, and lords no longer felt it desirable to ensure their income by lengthening the terms of leases, when frequent renegotiation of these could give them more opportunities to raise rents.

Such popular movements as occurred between 1381 and the early sixteenth century must be seen against this background, which goes far to explain their character. The grievances which prompted them tended not to be social, but political, fiscal, or even religious. The Lollard rising of Sir John Oldcastle in 1414 had no social aims; indeed the rebels do not appear to have had any programme at all, beyond a vague idea of seizing the King (without any very clear idea of what they would then do with him). The revolt was essentially Oldcastle's attempted revenge for his arrest in the previous year, and the only economic motive which can be discerned among some of the rebels was a possible hope of seizing some ecclesiastical property. The rising at Abingdon in 1431 (with off-shoots in the Midlands and London), which contemporaries associated with Lollardy, although on somewhat tenuous grounds, was undoubtedly anti-clerical, and some rebels seem to have put forward plans for ecclesiastical disestablishment.

They do not, however, seem to have possessed any programme for the betterment of lay society. Although both these revolts secured some support from fairly widespread areas, this was not strong, and they were easily suppressed.

Jack Cade's rising in 1450, which affected mainly Kent and various neighbouring counties, was a far more serious affair, and had repercussions over a much wider area. It marked the culmination of a series of political disorders, directed primarily against Henry VI's chief adviser, William de la Pole, duke of Suffolk. One of his associates, Adam Moleyns, bishop of Chichester, was murdered on 9 January, he himself was committed to the Tower on the demand of the Commons on 28 January and two sets of articles of impeachment were laid against him. Although he was pardoned by the King and sent into exile (presumably for his own protection), there were riots against him after his release from the Tower, and when he sailed from England he was intercepted and murdered on 2 May. De la Pole's unpopularity was essentially political and personal; he was associated with the failure of the war in France and was rightly suspected of exploiting royal favour in the interest of himself and his friends (Ch.22; 147, pp.44, 62). Popular unrest had begun to develop even before his death – commissions were appointed to investigate insurrections in Kent on 2 February and in Surrey on 11 April, and a London chronicle tells of the arrest and execution, at an unspecified date, of a rebel leader known as Bluebeard. (7; 22, p.158) By the end of May the Kentishmen were marching on London, in June there was a skirmish with royal forces, and they presented a formal complaint of their grievances. On 4 July they entered London, although the authorities there were able to reassert themselves more rapidly than in 1381. On the next day a pardon was offered to the rebels, who withdrew from the city, although their leader Cade remained under arms, putting himself outside the scope of the pardon, and was killed on 12 July. Another prominent man at court, the King's confessor, Bishop Ayscough of Salisbury, was murdered at Edington in Wiltshire on 29 June. The troubles in Kent dragged on sporadically for some two years; in August 1450 a certain William Parmenter virtually proclaimed himself Cade's successor by calling himself the second captain of Kent, in April 1451 there were troubles fomented by Henry Hasilden, and in May 1452 there was yet further disorder (42).

What was the cause of these disorders? The Kentishmen's statement of grievances, comprising fifteen articles and five requests to the King, throws some light on this (7; 11, pp.338–42) The first article stated that there were rumours that Kent was to be turned into a forest as a punishment for Suffolk's death. This rumour may have done what the poll tax did in 1381, set fire to a potentially explosive situation, indeed one which had already shown signs of bursting into flame. But it is clear that there were more fundamental problems. Complaints were then made about the exclusion of the lords of the King's blood from his Council, obviously an allusion to the duke of York, about purveyance of goods for the King's household, and about extortion by sheriffs and their officers. Allegations of treason were made concerning the loss of lands in France, a matter which may have particularly concerned the Kentishmen, whose vulnerability to raids was obvious, and who may well have been alarmed by the issue of a commission of array, and a command to set up warning beacons, on 14 April. Complaint was made that there was no free election of knights of the shire, and that those elected knights had taken bribes for appointing tax-collectors in it. The King was asked to take the duke of York into his counsel, to punish those responsible for the death of the duke of Gloucester and to end extortions, particularly those by four named persons.

Apart from one passing reference to the Statute of Labourers, social grievances do not appear in the petition. More important are the political demands, but most significant of all was local discontent at the action of royal officials in the shire. This was directed particularly at the sheriff, William Crowmer, and his father-in-law, Lord Say, who as Sir James Fiennes had been sheriff in 1442. Say had been Treasurer since 1449, so the attacks on him link local grievances with general hostility to the court. There is good reason to believe that these attacks were well justified, because after the defeat of the rising and Cade's death, a commission, sent into Kent to investigate extortions there, held inquests in various parts of the shire between late August and late October 1450. At these the jurors accused various officials, particularly those named in the complaint, of extortion, disseisin, forcible detention of goods and fabrication of warrants of arrest for the purpose of extorting money (42). In June too, after an attempt to repel the rebels had failed, and the leaders of the royal force, Sir Humphrey Stafford and William Stafford, had been killed at Sevenoaks, the government had tried to placate the Kentishmen by arresting Crowmer and Say and sending them to the Tower, and when Cade's men entered London in July, those two were among their earliest victims (16, p.192). The rebels also secured support in London from opponents of the court party. The courtiers' most prominent associate there was a draper, Philip Malpas, who had been chosen alderman of Lime Street ward in 1448 only through royal influence. His house was sacked during the revolt, and he himself was discharged from office; although he lived for almost twenty years more, he was not reappointed. Some of Cade's allies in the city were men of position, although the bulk of his support came from the poorer classes (128, pp.111, 115).

The evidence suggests that Cade's support was fairly widely based, and that the strength of his leadership lay in his ability to act as spokesmen for all the social groups which supported him. The revolt was not purely one of the agricultural classes, although a substantial number of those pardoned for participation in it are described as 'husbandman' or 'labourer'. A number of those involved were artisans from the Kentish towns, some of whom, particularly those connected with the cloth trade, may have had a special grievance, as a sharp decline in cloth exports after 1448 could well have caused local unemployment (66, pp.96–7). Even more striking as a pointer to the greater importance of political rather than social factors in the rebellion was the participation of men from higher up the social scale; over ninety participants are described as 'gentleman' or 'esquire', and there was even one knight in the list of those pardoned, Sir William Trussel of Aylmesthorpe, Leicestershire. It is not clear how far there were similar local grievances to those of the Kentishmen in some of the other shires which were involved in the revolt, notably Sussex and Surrey, although it is probable that the resentment of the citizens of Salisbury at the powers which the bishop exercised there may have been one factor behind the murder of Ayscough (7; 147, pp.63, 66–8).

As a leader, Cade was able to maintain discipline among his men, at least until they reached London, and his success in defeating the force sent against him argues that he possessed some military capacity. Possibly there was some break-down of control when he entered London, which may well have contributed to a reaction against him on the part of the citizens. The attack on Malpas's house certainly seems to have alarmed them and led them to co-operate with the author-ities against the rebels (22, p.161).

As in 1381 there was no specific disloyalty to the King – hatred was concen-trated on his advisers. This raises a further problem, whether or not there was, as some Tudor writers believed, Yorkist influence behind the rising. Certainly Cade's assumption of the name Mortimer, by which he was known in the earlier stages of the revolt, hints at Yorkist connections. (Indeed he was pardoned under that name, and the discovery that it was a false one provided an additional pretext for its revocation.) But Richard of York himself made no attempt to co-ordinate his movements with Cade's, and the demands for his inclusion among the King's advisers probably do no more than reflect dislike of the existing court faction.

It is worth spending considerable time in examining the causes of the 1450 rebellion, because they contrast markedly with those of the 1381 revolt. Cade and his supporters had no constructive programme for social reform, and appeared to be unconcerned about questions of servile status or land rents. Such economic grievances as existed were probably prompted by such immediate issues as the slump in the cloth industry rather than by long-term agrarian questions. The major grievances were political, although not necessarily dynastic, and reflected discontent at the abuse of power by the men who controlled the government. The rising, the most extensive popular movement between 1381 and the sixteenth cen-tury, was relatively limited in its aims and was certainly not directed at the over-throw of the social order.

During the Yorkist period there were undoubtedly some movements of pop-ular discontent; in 1471 the Essex men seem to have joined Fauconberg's attack on London because they felt that the citizens were paying insufficient prices for dairy supplies. A late and rather unreliable source also explained some of the northern discontent in 1469 as the result of the demands of the Hospital of St Leonard at York for payments of sheaves from the northern counties (13, p.121; 40, p.218). But neither of these cases really proves the existence of strong agrarian unrest; both show that local discontent could be drawn into the political struggles of contending dynasties and their magnate supporters.

In the early Tudor period, the main occasions for insurrections seem to have been fiscal. Two risings under Henry VII followed attempts to levy taxes; in 1489 the earl of Northumberland lost his life at the hands of a force of rebellious York-shiremen when he was trying to collect the subsidy granted that year, and in 1497 the levying of a tax for a war with Scotland led to a more serious revolt in Corn-wall. According to one account, the Cornishmen felt that the affairs of the North were too remote to interest them. A substantial army marched on London, and although it was defeated and the leaders were put to death, to do so the King had to divert the force which was being prepared for the campaign in Scotland (73, pp.14–16).

Resistance to taxation was not always so violent. In 1513 there was opposition to a tax imposition in Yorkshire – indeed on this occasion a remission of assessment was granted on grounds of poverty, so the government seems to have been prepared to meet genuine grievances. A decade later, there was a more serious crisis. There was opposition to a subsidy demand in 1523, and when in 1525 Henry VIII and Cardinal Wolsey attempted to levy the so-called Amicable Grant, to finance a campaign against France, they faced serious resistance. The demand was heavy, for a payment of one-sixth on the goods of the laity and of one-third on those of the clergy, and some men refused payment outright, while others put forward the plea that they could not afford to pay. The most serious trouble was in Suffolk, in the cloth-manufacturing area of Lavenham and Sudbury, where the dukes of Norfolk and Suffolk claimed that they were faced with a body of 4,000 men, who alleged that they had no work and did not know how to get their living. In fact, even in this area where the textile trade was important, such a high level of unemployment would have been surprising, for cloth exports in the mid 1520s were substantially higher than earlier in the decade, when there had been a marked recession. The authorities approached the crisis cautiously; in Suffolk the dukes arrested only the four principal offenders, and even they were pardoned when they were brought before the Star Chamber (66, pp.115–16; 73, pp.17–19). In these rebellions, the main grievances voiced were fiscal, although it is not certain how far the taxation itself was the real cause of discontent and how far merely the last straw which could not be borne in a time when land was becoming scarce and real wages were in decline [A.1].

Certainly by the second quarter of the sixteenth century there were serious social grievances which underlie such movements as the Pilgrimage of Grace of 1536 and the West Country and Norfolk revolts of 1549. Although detailed consideration of these lies beyond the scope of the present book,[1] it is worth noting that they raised more specifically social and economic grievances than the risings of the fifteenth century. Enclosure of common land, invasion of common rights and engrossing of farms were among the complaints put forward in the Norfolk rising, and there was also a demand for the ending of serfdom, although there is little evidence that there were still many men of villein status. The western rising was prompted largely by religious conservatism, although an attempt to limit the number of servants a gentleman might have had social overtones (73, p.61, 69, 136, 142–4). The most complex of the risings was the Pilgrimage of Grace, the problems of which have been covered in two important papers, both of which stress the varying motives of the participants (68; 69). In the end, the rising should probably be seen primarily as religious and political in character, although certain sectors of it, notably those in Westmorland and Craven, were concerned with such agrarian matters as enclosures and the rate of entry fines. It is possible that here, and again in Norfolk in 1549, the basic grievances lay in local rather than national conditions.

Nevertheless, it seems fair to say that by the 1530s social grievances were again being voiced to an extent that they had not been in the previous century. Behind this, almost certainly, lay the new economic pressures of an expanding population which were leaving the agricultural worker worse off than he had been in the years of land surplus. The balance of power was shifting back to favour the landlord, and it was to remain that way for a long time.

---

1. They will be considered more fully in volume II of this series, A. G. R. Smith, *The Emergence of a Nation State*.

CHAPTER 5

Enclosures and depopulation

Among the grievances of some of the rural rebels in the sixteenth century were complaints about the enclosure of lands by lords – this occurred in the north-west sector of the Pilgrimage of Grace, and the casting down of hedges marked the start of the Norfolk rising of 1549. In the 1540s, furthermore, there was a considerable quantity of writing denouncing the practice (44, pp.941–53). Criticism of it was by no means new: a generation earlier, in the second decade of the century, there had been various anti-enclosure measures, an Act in 1515 to prevent the conversion of land from tillage to pasture, and the establishment of commissions of enquiry by Wolsey in 1517 and 1518 to investigate the extent of enclosures. The returns of these commissions, together with subsequent proceedings throughout the cardinal's chancellorship against those who had broken the Act, provide much of the evidence on the whole process. At almost the same time (1516), Thomas More, in his *Utopia*, wrote the most famous of all denunciations of the evils of enclosure:

> Forsooth, my lord, quoth I, your sheep that were wont to be so meek and tame and so small eaters, now, I hear say, be become so great devourers and so wild, that they eat up and swallow down the very men themselves. They consume, destroy, and devour whole fields, houses and cities. For look in what parts of the realm doth grow the finest and dearest wool, there noblemen and gentlemen, yea and certain abbots . . . leave no ground for tillage. They enclose all pastures; they throw down houses; they pluck down towns, and leaving nothing standing but only the church to be made into a sheep-house . . . the husbandmen be thrust out of their own, or else by covin and fraud or by violent oppression they be put besides it, or by wrongs and injuries they be so wearied, that they be compelled to sell all. By one means, therefore, or by other, either by hook or crook, they must needs depart away, poor, silly, wretched souls, men, women, husbands, wives, fatherless children, widows, woeful mothers with their young babes, and their whole household small in substance and much in number, as husbandry requireth many hands. Away they trudge, I say, out of their known and accustomed houses, finding no place to rest in.

More's eloquence has set the tone for much historical writing on the subject, but while one should not deny that enclosures created a good deal of suffering, one should also remember that More was exaggerating his points for the sake of effect. Not only that, he concentrated his attack purely on enclosures as a cause of depopulation, and by so doing both failed to consider how far enclosures might have been the result rather than the cause, and omitted to mention a related question, that of the 'engrossing' or accumulation of farms by a single owner. This could be combined with enclosure, but was not necessarily identical with it. Farms could be accumulated without being enclosed, and individual yeomen could, by exchanging strips in the open fields with their neighbours, consolidate their holdings and thereby create a unit which was easier to work. Such consolidation was indeed commended by contemporary writers on agriculture. More serious was the danger to a community when enclosure by a lord took in parts of the common land, on which the villagers had relied to graze their own stock. Indeed grazing rights could be an issue in themselves, and disputes over these probably made a major contribution to bringing about the Norfolk rebellion of 1549 (73, pp.71, 142–3).

The government's motive in attacking enclosures was not simply disinterested concern for justice for the poor, although Wolsey may have been anxious about their welfare. The Crown's interest was above all the defence of the land rather than of villagers' property rights. As early as 1488–89, an Act dealing with the Isle of Wight declared that it had been made desolate by being turned into pasture, and that it could not long be defended from the King's enemies. More specifically, it attacked engrossing of holdings and provided penalties for this. In the following year a general Act condemned depopulation (although not engrossing as such), declaring that in towns where previously 200 persons were occupied, there were now only two or three herdsmen, and the rest were fallen into idleness. The same themes were reechoed in the second decade of the sixteenth century, when the government again began to take an interest in restraining enclosure, and attempted, sometimes successfully, to restore land from pasture to tillage. There were further measures in the 1530s; an Act of 1533 attempted to limit the size of the flock that one man might own and to prevent the engrossing of holdings and another in 1536 authorized the King to proceed against any encloser of land converted from tillage since 1488 (58, pp.104–6, 110–11). As the Act was largely confined to the Midlands (with the addition of Cambridgeshire and the Isle of Wight), it is unlikely that the motive of securing the defence of the realm bulked as large as in 1488–89. The aim of the measure may also have been financial, because the Crown was empowered to distrain for half of the profits resulting from the enclosure; it was not, however, an easy way to raise money, so it is unlikely to have been the only reason for the Act.

The proceedings taken under these Acts provide many of the known facts concerning enclosures and depopulation. A major defence by many of those prosecuted was that the enclosures had taken place before the practice had been made an offence, and although the practice continued after this date there is good reason to believe that this was often the case. John Hales of Coventry, a bitter opponent of enclosures, wrote in 1549 that the bulk of them had occurred before the accession of Henry VII, and the Italian historian Polydore Vergil (probably writing about 1530), said of the proceedings of 1517, that for half a century or more previously, sheep-farming nobles had tried to find devices to increase the income of their lands, and that to this end they had destroyed dwelling-houses and filled up the land with animals. Even more important is the testimony of the fifteenth-century Warwick chantry priest John Rous, who died in 1491. In his *Historia Regum Angliae* (generally a work of little value) there is an isolated and indignant digression on current depopulation in his own shire, prompted by his description of the harrying of villages by William the Conqueror. He names fifty-eight depopulated villages, almost all of which can be identified. Indeed, Rous claimed that he had petitioned Parliament in 1459 asking for legislation on enclosures, and although no such petition is preserved, there is one from as early as 1414 from the village of Chesterton in Cambridgeshire referring to depopulation there (19, pp.276–7; 58, pp.81–2, 102–3, 148).

It is clear from this that periods when enclosure was taking place do not necessarily correspond with those when articulate protests were being voiced against them. Why this was the case we shall return to later; for the moment our concern must be with the chronology, distribution and causes of the enclosures themselves. The problems connected with these are inseparable, because of the variety of local conditions, which led to them taking place at different times in various parts of the kingdom. In parts of the West Country and the South, much of the land had been enclosed long before the fifteenth century, whereas in some of the northern counties the movement did not get under way until late in the sixteenth. In Lincolnshire and the East Riding of Yorkshire, a substantial number of villages disappeared from the records in the late fourteenth and early fifteenth centuries, as well as in the second half of the fifteenth century, which seems to have been the worst period of depopulation in the area most seriously affected in the Midlands, particularly in Northamptonshire, Oxfordshire, Warwickshire, Buckinghamshire, Leicestershire and Nottinghamshire (58, pp.170–3, 220–1, 229).

Local conditions must go a long way to explaining why some villages were vulnerable to enclosure and others were not, and these variations could occur within the limits of a single shire. Although Devon is a long way from the most seriously affected areas of enclosure, it does provide well-documented evidence of such variations. In the east of the shire, there was some enclosure as early as the 1250s, it was well under way by the middle of the fourteenth century and virtually complete by the mid fifteenth. In the south of the county, it was only beginning on some manors in the late fourteenth and early fifteenth, while on others it did not occur until the sixteenth and seventeenth. The areas enclosed in the south of the county were on average larger than those in the east, so it is likely that enclosure there took place at a time when conditions were more conducive to the practice. The study of two villages, one from each part of the shire, makes it clear why this was the case. Pressure on land was fairly slack in the south (most obviously shown by the fact that when holdings were reoccupied they were often taken up by men who already held land, and not by landless men), whereas in the east there was no shortage of tenants, and the demand for land was maintained.

These distinctions in Devon are fairly clear, and should warn the historian not to simplify the picture by thinking overmuch in broad regional terms. The basic character of husbandry in a particular locality was a major factor in determining its vulnerability to the encloser. Areas of forest, where the villages already had little arable farming, were relatively immune, even in shires which were otherwise seriously affected: this can be seen in Charnwood Forest in Leicestershire and the Forest of Arden in Warwickshire. Similarly, there is little evidence of desertion in areas which had been reclaimed from marshland (58, map facing p.228, p.231).

If one works back from the sixteenth-century evidence, one is left with a strong impression that the years after 1450 saw the greatest pressure of enclosures. Detailed evidence is scarce, although recent archaelogical investigation has succeeded in identifying many deserted villages, and it is to be hoped that gradually excavation may help to clarify, at least within broad limits, when some of these desertions occurred. A more precise source for this than archaeology is the record of tax assessments, and more particularly the grants of tax relief which were made in the fifteenth-century reassessments. The basis of payment was the subsidy assessment of 1334, but although this remained in use for the following two centuries, the variations in the extent to which relief was granted in the fifteenth century to communities which had declined in size and wealth since that date suggest that a genuine effort was made to judge their capacity to pay at particular times. An important conclusion that can be drawn from the fiscal records is that the immediate effect of the Black Death in 1348–49 was slight in destroying communities, because most of the villages which eventually disappeared are still recorded as contributing to subsidies levied in the fifteenth century. There may have been a few villages abandoned in the aftermath of the plague, particularly those on poorer soil, as their inhabitants moved to better lands to take up holdings which had fallen vacant. Here it was a combination of the fall in population and local soil conditions which killed a village rather than the plague alone. If there had been land-hunger comparable to the pre-plague period, it is unlikely that the villages would have disappeared (58, pp.160–2, 209).

These factors must bulk larger in the explanation of depopulation than the sixteenth-century writers' scapegoat, the rapacious landlords. Depopulation from plague was a very real factor in the long term, and while it might not destroy a village immediately, it could weaken it as a social and economic unit. This raises another difficulty for the historian, because it is far harder to estimate the extent to which a village had shrunk or when this occurred than to note when it'was finally deserted. Desertion could be marked by its disappearance from the taxation rolls, or by the union of the parish with another, whereas decay could only be hinted at by a relief of tax payments. For example, Riseholme, near Lincoln, did not finally disappear until the late sixteenth century – ecclesiastical records show that it still existed in the 1520s, but that by 1575 it had no facilities for burials. The earliest specific reference to its desertion comes from 1602. In 1428, however, it and some neighbouring villages were excused from paying the subsidy because it had less than ten households, and the excavation of one of the houses suggests that it had been deserted as early as the second half of the fourteenth century.

The case of Riseholme illustrates clearly how the casualties occurred in small settlements rather than in more substantial ones. The 1334 tax assessments and the 1377 poll-tax returns show which communities existed at those dates (the latter also showing how few had disappeared between them), and make it clear that a high proportion of those which eventually disappeared were markedly below the average size (58, pp.162–3, 207). The tax remissions of the first half of the fifteenth century show that some of the villages which later disappeared were granted substantial reliefs, although this was not universal. Unfortunately, the survival of tax records from the middle years of the century (and more especially after 1450) is more patchy than from the period immediately before, so it is not always possible to trace the disappearance of villages at precisely the time when a substantial number of the desertions seems to have occurred.

The sixteenth-century writers who condemned depopulation looked for a depopulator, and found him in the enclosing landlord, who found that stock-rearing was more profitable than corn-growing. There are some pointers to this being an accurate judgement, although the period for which wool and corn prices have been studied in detail does not go further back than 1490, and therefore does not include what are probably the most serious years of enclosure (58, p.183). However, the evidence is not entirely conclusive, and in a period when lords were having difficulty in finding tenants to take up holdings, it may well be that the conversion from arable to grazing was forced on them. The raising of sheep could bring some profit, while leaving land vacant could bring none. Furthermore, even if a surplus of wool was produced, there was perhaps more hope of selling it to the developing cloth industry than of disposing of grain which was not required, as a demand for clothing can be more flexible than one for food when men have additional purchasing power (59; 62). This is not to deny that there were unscrupulous landlords who were guilty of depopulation – the evidence that there were is clear. The danger is to exaggerate their importance, as it seems clear that their actions tended to give the final blow to communities which were already in decay rather than to destroy those which were flourishing.

The lord's power to remove the inhabitants of a village varied from place to place. Where a large number of the villagers were freeholders, they could more easily resist the lord's attempts at enclosure than where their numbers were low. Significantly, the villages which tended to disappear were those with a low proportion of peasant proprietors (83, p.28). When the tenants were copyholders, much might depend on the precise custom by which they held their land (Ch.4). Where tenure was for life only, and not by inheritance, where entry fines were not fixed by custom, it was possible for the lord, perfectly legally, to raise these to a level which a possible heir could not pay, not in the expectation of getting more money, but in the certainty that failure to pay would give him the right to evict. The process of enclosures thus illustrates the limits to the security obtained by copyholders.

In 1466 a Bohemian visitor to England commented: '. . . the peasants dig ditches round their fields and meadows and so fence them in that no one can pass on foot or on horseback except by the main roads' (25, p.53). This should remind us that not all enclosures were made by the land-owning class, but could be the work of the peasants themselves. One point, however, should be borne in mind. The Bohemian party saw only a limited part of the country, landing in Kent, and travelling via London to Reading, Salisbury and Poole, whence they sailed to France. The main areas of depopulation and enclosure in the Midlands were not on their itinerary, and in Kent, where the peasant community was free, it may well have been the peasantry who wished to consolidate their holdings. The other shires which the Bohemians visited, namely Berkshire, Hampshire and Wiltshire, were also in fact ones which were comparatively little affected by enclosures (58, pp.339–40, 351–3, 389–91).

Fifteenth-century agriculture, as we have seen (Ch.2), gave the peasantry opportunities to consolidate their holdings, and it may well be that this led to a decline in the traditional co-operative cultivation of the open-field communities, as men purchased their own draught animals and ploughs. For such men, enclosure of their lands could be the next step (62), and it is worth remembering that even John Hales, the mid-sixteenth-century opponent of enclosures, was prepared to admit that enclosure *per se* was not necessarily evil: his particular concern was with the turning of arable fields into pasture (58, p.180). Peasant enclosures, however, were not so likely to do this as those by greater men, whose lands were sufficiently extensive for them to support large flocks and who would therefore have found such a conversion of land usage economically worth while.

Despite suggestions in the preamble to a draft bill of 1514, that the men responsible for the enclosures were townsmen and speculators who were buying up land, it is clear from the evidence of the subsequent proceedings that the offenders were very largely drawn from old-established families of nobility and gentry. Indeed, the evidence goes far to bear out the criticisms made by More in *Utopia*. The evidence for Leicestershire, which had been very fully studied, shows that between 1485 and 1550, 2.1 per cent of the total enclosure was the responsibility of the Crown, 17.6 per cent that of the monasteries, 12.1 per cent that of the nobility and 67.5 per cent that of the gentry (58, pp.105, 190–1; 82, p.71).[1] There were variations in detail from shire to shire, but the predominant part played by the existing land-owning families seems to have been common.

To put these actions into perspective, however, one must remember that enclosures were by no means complete. If one again looks at Leicestershire, one sees that at most one-tenth of the open-field arable was enclosed, and this in one of the counties which was most seriously affected (82, p.69). Nor need an entire village be affected. At Cotesbach in the same county, about thirty people, from five households, were evicted about 1501, and the lands affected represented about a fifth of the manor. The rest of it remained open until the early seventeenth century, when new enclosures led to major agrarian unrest in the shire, with Cotesbach at the centre of it.

One major problem remains: if, as seems clear was the case, the main period of depopulation in the mid fifteenth century preceded public hostility to enclosures, why was there a sudden growth of the latter from the second decade of the sixteenth century onwards? The writing of *Utopia* and Wolsey's proceedings mark the start of a period in which enclosure was vigorously condemned by some, although still practised by others. There had been little sign of such popular sentiment at the time of the earlier enclosure – the attitude of John Rous cannot be matched elsewhere. Possibly the answer to this question may be found in the recovery of population, and the renewal of pressure on available land. If, as recent work has suggested (Ch.1), the sustained growth of population from the doldrums of the fifteenth century began to affect the economy in the early years of the sixteenth century rather than previously, this would come close to the period when the volume of criticism of enclosures became more vocal and more explicit. The comparative absence of protest in the fifteenth century may be explained simply by the fact that depopulation was less of a social problem, and that if a lord evicted tenants, they still had a reasonable prospect of finding land elsewhere. By the early sixteenth century, vacant holdings were again being taken up, and the level of rents and entry fines was rising; all of these changes reflect increasing demand for land (59). In consequence, enclosure of arable was now creating more social problems than it could solve. In the fifteenth century it had been a practical way of making agriculture more profitable, in the sixteenth it was more likely to create a vagrancy problem as men were dispossessed from the land, and this indeed was a social issue which came to the forefront of public attention in the Tudor period. It may well have been the realization that this was the case which led to the emergence of criticism of those responsible for enclosures.

---

1. Hoskins does not account for the remaining 0.7 per cent but states that peasantry and merchants do not feature among the enclosers.

CHAPTER 6

Urban society and economy

Throughout the Middle Ages, the bulk of the population lived in the country, but although, comparatively speaking, the number of town dwellers was small, they played a considerable part in the national economy. They were largely responsible for overseas trade, and the towns provided centres for the regional economy of their own part of the country. They were closely linked with this, and in some cases it is clear that the growth or decline of a town resulted from economic changes in the surrounding rural area. Generalizations about the state of the towns in late medieval England are, however, risky; each had its own history, which might be very different from that of its neighbour, and it is likely that even when more individual studies have been made of particular towns the general picture will be one of diversity rather than of similarity. Even when one can see a similar history of decline or recovery, this did not necessarily occur in different towns at the same time (71).

There certainly is scope for such studies: documentary material survives in town archives in such forms as deeds and rentals, and in some cases it can be supplemented by archaeological work, as twentieth-century redevelopment in town centres has given opportunities to investigate the surviving material remains below. Although such rescue excavation work cannot be more than piecemeal, as sites become available, results already obtained have provided useful information on conditions of urban life, in the types of buildings where people lived, on the desertion of houses within towns and around them, and on the distribution of trades within the towns. Unsocial crafts, such as butchering and tanning, were assigned to particular quarters, and those with a high fire risk, pottery-making or blacksmith work, were excluded from the more densely populated areas (90, pp.47–8).

Historians have taken two main approaches, the legal and the economic, to the urban history of the Middle Ages. The former is concerned with the government and status of the boroughs, and their relations with the Crown and the units of local government within which they existed, the latter with the structure of society within them and their changing economic fortunes. The earlier approach is in some ways simpler, in that one can tell precisely what was and what was not a borough, because a borough was created by charter in a formal legal act. For the same reason, it can be misleading, because not all centres of population which possessed recognizably urban characteristics, as for example the employment of the inhabitants in manufacturing or trade rather than in agriculture, were boroughs in the strict legal sense. The degree of economic specialization might vary from one centre to another, and in the last resort it is not always easy to define what was a town. Although most of the greater towns were boroughs, some major centres of manufacture, such as the cloth-making villages of Lavenham and Hadleigh, were not. Irrespective of their legal status, however, they should clearly be considered as towns in any discussion of the urban economy.

Undoubtedly the population crisis of the mid fourteenth century hit the towns severely. Insanitary conditions, and the concentration of people and rats in a limited area, made them vulnerable to attacks of plague, and it is noteworthy that even when the disease had ceased to be common in the country, it persisted in urban areas. Studies of individual towns suggest that they were severely hit, that properties were deserted and that in some cases parishes had to be united, as the existing ones were too poor to maintain the services of the Church (77, pp.286–8). Many towns had to rely on immigration from the country to maintain even a reduced level of population, and the easing of pressure of population on the land in the country reduced the urge on men to move, although as we have seen in our examination of rural society men did continue to leave the land to escape the burdens of serfdom (70; 104, pp.206–10; Ch.4). The plague may not, however, have been solely responsible for urban decay, as there are few signs of the expansion of suburbs in English towns between 1300 and the end of the Middle Ages, and at Oxford there are references to houses falling into decay as early as 1340.

London was the greatest town in England, and during the fourteenth and fifteenth centuries its economic resources increased more markedly than those of most other parts of the country. The 1377 poll-tax returns suggest that it was over three times the size of the largest provincial centres, Bristol and York, almost five times that of Coventry and six times that of Norwich (104, p.1). Tax returns of the 1520s do not provide an exact comparison, as they are concerned with the wealth rather than the number of the inhabitants, but they show its continued pre-eminence, almost ten times as wealthy as Norwich, and over fifteen times as wealthy as Bristol (82, pp.13–14). The fiscal evidence also points to an increase in its wealth in relation to the country as a whole: between 1334 and 1515 the assessed wealth of the city increased fifteenfold in absolute terms, and from 2 per cent to 8.9 per cent of the assessed wealth of the nation as a whole (101). Even Continental visitors were impressed by the city: a Bohemian visitor in 1466 described it as large and magnificent, with beautiful churches, in 1483 the Italian Dominic Mancini said that it was famous throughout the world, and in 1497 another Italian visitor laid stress on the wealth of its citizens. Both Italian writers commented particularly on the number of goldsmiths' shops in the city (3, pp.101–5; 25, pp.51–2; 35, pp.42–3). The anonymous writer of 1497 said that apart from London there were only two towns of importance in the country, Bristol and York, but in this he was misinformed, as it seems likely that Norwich, which had undoubtedly had a period of difficulties in the early fifteenth century, had begun to recover about 1465 or 1470, and was on the way to becoming the second wealthiest city in the land, as it was in the 1520s.

The dominance of London may partly reflect the decline of other centres, particularly in the South and South-east, and indeed London merchants may sometimes have been responsible for this. This was probably true of Southampton, towards the middle of Henry VIII's reign, although the city's decline may have been foreshadowed by earlier events. Its importance in the fifteenth century was connected with its position as the centre of Italian trade in England, but the Florentine galleys disappeared from the port after 1478 and the Venetians after 1509. The last years of Henry VII had been a prosperous period for the port – the average annual sum paid in customs dues from 1504 to 1509 was over £10,000, and in the early years of Henry VIII a group of merchants had maintained voyages to Brazil. But although trade passed through Southampton, it was not necessarily merchants of the town who were handling it. Londoners were deeply involved in the revival of the Gascon wine trade in Edward IV's reign, and also in the trade in metals, particularly Cornish tin. Improvements in shipping and the foundation of the guild of pilots of Trinity House (incorporated in 1541) made for safer navigation in the Thames, and the London merchants removed their trade nearer home. By the latter part of Henry VIII's reign the quantity of trade, as measured by customs payments, had shrunk catastrophically, to an average of just over £2,000 annually in 1535–40 and to about £663 annually in 1541–45. Although John Leland in the 1530s described a town apparently prosperous from the condition of its buildings, these may well have been erected before the decline set in.

The factors which determined the fortunes of individual towns varied. The worst case of decline, that of Boston, was brought about by the decline of the wool trade, on the export of which it had grown, and its failure to secure any substantial share of cloth exports. The Midlands cloth industry, centred on Coventry, had originally used Boston as an outlet, but by the fifteenth century was exporting mainly through London, and Coventry itself was also in decline. In the North Sea trade too, Boston had been the victim of the growing power of the German Hanse. Hull, too, suffered from the poor relations between England and the Hanse in the second half of the fifteenth century, and this may have been one factor which affected the trade of York, which had used Hull as a centre for exports. The value of York's trade at Hull probably fell from about £10,000 annually to about £2,500 between the last quarter of the fourteenth century and the middle of the sixteenth (56). In this last case there is no reason to believe that there was any direct influence of London which contributed to the decline.

Some towns, however, were able to prosper – Colchester, Salisbury and Newcastle among the larger ones, Exeter, Plymouth, Reading and Ipswich among the smaller ones – and it is likely that their prosperity depended on local factors, more particularly increasing activity in cloth manufacturing and exports, which affected the towns of the West Country and in Suffolk. Newcastle's success is less easy to explain, for as late as the early sixteenth century its main export commodity was wool, although by the reign of Henry VIII it seems to have expanded its trade in coal, iron and lead (59; 71; 75, p.45).

The dominance of London in the country has been reflected in the interests of historians, who have devoted more time to it than to provincial centres, although recent work has done something to redress the balance. It must, however, still bulk large in any examination of English urban life, not only because many of its characteristics were common to it and other towns, but also because they can be most fully studied there. Notably, one sees the dominance of a comparatively small oligarchical group of great merchants, drawn from a limited circle of the major companies. This had been consolidated in power by the end of the fourteenth century, after the one serious attempt to overthrow it. The leader of this, the draper John Northampton, although himself a member of one of the greatest companies, joined forces with the lesser guilds to try to break the control of a small group of dominant capitalists, particularly those in the victualling guilds of the fishmongers, grocers and vintners. In 1376, following the Good Parliament, in which one of the oligarchs, the alderman Richard Lyons, had been impeached, a new system was introduced by electing the city council, by crafts instead of wards. Though there may have been some hostility between the victuallers and the non-victuallers, this can hardly have been the only factor involved. For one thing, the victuallers were never able to secure a majority on the council, and for another, a substantial number of the men in the victualling guilds had other interest – grocers and fishmongers were among the most important wool exporters at this period and one does not know how far individuals actually practised the trade of their own guild – so it may have been less in their interest than has sometimes been thought to keep food prices high (84, pp.251–3; 104, pp.77–80; 109). The struggle is probably better understood as one between a dominant oligarchy and those whom they excluded from power. Until 1381 the greater merchants contrived to maintain their influence in the court of aldermen, but after the Peasants' Revolt Northampton was able to capture the mayoralty, and may have exploited the fears aroused by this disorder to try to inculpate his opponents. Certainly the five aldermen accused of collaboration with the rebels were all drawn from the victualling guilds (11, p.212). Some two years later, however, the old ruling group recovered control, election by wards was restored, and the greater men in each were again able to dominate affairs. Even the attempt to limit the number of members each guild or craft might have on the council did not curb the power of the greater companies. (104, p.79, Table 6). In the fifteenth century London remained under merchant rule: all but 6 of the 88 men who were mayor during it were drawn from the 6 greatest companies, the mercers, grocers, drapers, fishmongers, goldsmiths and skinners. The same 6 companies furnished 148 out of 173 aldermen during the same period. The first 3 of them were the most important, supplying between them 61 of the mayors and 105 of the aldermen (128, pp.107; 109).

The London merchants of this period do not, however, represent a closely connected group of families as they had done in an earlier age: the civic upper class was constantly being renewed, either as families died out, or as successful men moved out from the city to the country. It has been estimated that the majority of the great London families survived there for no more than three generations in the male line, and it was certainly rare for men to prefer city life to that of the country (104, p.205). Between 1370 and 1500 there is only one case of a father and son both being aldermen, William Reynwell (1397–1403) and his son John (1416–45) (104, pp.363–4), although there are cases when brothers or cousins both held office. Among the most prominent London citizens of the period, those who were elected mayor more than once, only a minority were of certain London origin, such as Thomas Knolles (1399–1400, 1410–11), Nicholas Wotton (1415–16, 1430–31) and Henry Barton (1416–17, 1428–29). By comparison, Richard Whittington, who was unique in holding the office thrice (1397–98,

1406–7, 1419–20), came from a minor landed family in Gloucestershire. Robert Chichele (1411–12, 1421–22) came from Higham Ferrers in Northamptonshire where his father was a burgess, although he had a family connection with London through his mother. The family was clearly influential, perhaps having been helped by his brother who was archbishop of Canterbury, and a third brother was an alderman, although he never became mayor. Stephen Broun (1438–39, 1448–49) William Estfield (1429–30, 1437–38) came respectively from Newcastle and Yorkshire, Richard Lee (1460–1, 1469–70) and John Tate (1497–98, 1504) from Worcester and Coventry (104, pp.321–77).

It is almost always difficult to discover how these men built their fortunes at the beginning, because they leave no significant mark in the records until they have already made some mark in society. There is no reason to believe that the incomers brought any large amount of capital with them, although some may have had help at the start from their families. It is hardly likely that this could have been true of the greatest of them, Whittington, because his father had died with his estate encumbered by an outlawry incurred in a plea of debt. In many cases a man made his way by individual enterprise, in others a family grew in standing from one generation to the next, with the early stages of its ascent passing unnoticed. In the case of the Reynwells, mentioned earlier, the father had begun in the lesser guild of the girdlers, and transferred to the ironmongers, while the son was a member of the great company of the fishmongers. Sometimes one sees a family moving between associated crafts: the vintners and grocers could recruit from families in the lesser victualling trades, and workers in base metals might progress to being goldsmiths (104, p.222).

It is hard to judge how far the fluidity of the London ruling class is parallelled in other towns, or whether provincial towns preserved a more closely knit society. There is scope for more work on this, but already there are tentative pointers to the picture being similar. Urban dynasties in the English towns of which studies have been made were generally short-lived, seldom surviving beyond the third generation. Many of the prominent citizens, when their origins can be traced, were drawn from the lesser landed class, who may have given them moral or financial support. At York, admissions to the freedom of the city show that in the period 1301–1550 less than one-seventh of those admitted were drawn from citizen stock, while at Romney in Kent between 1433 and 1523, a quarter of the freemen came from outside the county, and only a third from within a 5-mile radius of the town (70).

Intermarriage between members of well-connected families could at any particular time create ties between them, and have repercussions in city politics. Besides marriage, other social ties drew men together; they could serve as godparents to the others' children, or as executors of their wills. In Southampton in the 1450s, when there was considerable bitterness in civic politics over the attitude to be taken to aliens, whether they should be welcomed for bringing wealth to the town, or attacked as intruders, marriage could lead a man to switch his allegiance from one group to another. Here too, however, there is impermanence in the city ruling class: while families such as the Fetplaces and Jameses were important for more than one generation, by the early Tudor period new names appear among the ruling oligarchy, Thomas Thomas and his son Sampson, John Dawtry and Richard Palshid. While the older families derived their wealth from trade, the newer ones drew it more from investment in property, after coming to prominence initially through service to the Crown, as controllers of customs or victuallers for armies, or by serving as town clerk. Possibly the declining part played by the merchant families in town government reflects a fall in their economic power.

Oligarchy was normal in most civic government, but was often achieved only after periods of tension. In fourteenth-century Norwich, the normal assembly was not democratic, but was limited to the 'better and more discreet' of the city. In 1404 the city obtained the right to have a mayor, but this was followed by conflicts, and in 1417 a new charter was granted, which established a civic constitution. The commonalty were allowed a council of sixty, which had to assent to the decisions of the mayor and aldermen, who took over the powers of the earlier assembly of twenty-four. Later in the century there were minor changes, of which the most important was the exclusion of the general body of the commonalty from electing the mayor and sheriffs in 1447. This constitution survived with only slight modifications until the Municipal Reform Act of 1835. Similar closed bodies were established elsewhere, as at Leicester and Northampton in 1489. In some places and at different times there was some resistance, at Lincoln at the end of the fourteenth century and at Southampton, where the mayor from 1488 to 1491 made an unsuccessful attempt to preserve some semblance of democracy (77, pp.259–61). The difficulty for the historian is that evidence for how councillors were elected is often lacking, and one does not know how many freemen could participate in choosing them, nor when membership of councils came to be filled by the choice of the existing councillors. By the early sixteenth century it is clear that oligarchies were often well established: other towns where this was the case included such major centres as Bristol, Exeter and Lynn (82, pp.101–2). It was similar in the smaller towns, as can be seen from examples in Sussex and Buckinghamshire. A small group of wealthy men were responsible for the day-to-day management of community affairs, and owned a disproportionate share of the property – some 40 per cent being owned by only 5 per cent of the inhabitants.

A characteristic development in the boroughs was the practice of incorporation. This gave the borough a corporate personality at law, with the right to sue and be sued, and also empowered it to exclude the shire officials and be directly responsible to the central government. The first town to acquire this status was Bristol in 1373, and others followed, York in 1396, Newcastle in 1400, Norwich in 1404 and Lincoln in 1409. The most elaborate of the charters of incorporation was that granted to Hull in 1440. A crucial factor in the development was the growth of property-owning by towns, probably so that rent income could compensate for deficiencies of toll revenue. In the 1391 Statute of Mortmain there is mention of towns acquiring property, and the Act virtually assumes that towns already possessed a corporate and perpetual identity, although few boroughs had as yet received formal recognition of their corporate status. This mortmain legislation was followed by their being licensed to acquire lands and rents (90, pp.140–6).

Rents did not, however, necessarily solve the difficulties of town finance. The levels and movements of urban rent are hard to document, but where substantial series of records survive, it is clear that in some towns at any rate, rents fell in the fifteenth century. York provides interesting evidence, though in view of the city's declining cloth industry, it may be dangerous to regard it as typical of towns in general. In the late fourteenth century, between 1371 and 1401 when rural rents were declining, the number of tenements owned by the vicars-choral of the Minster increased from 183 to 238, and the average rent rose from 6.7 to 7.1s., an increase of just under 6 per cent. There is no particular reason to believe that this was caused merely by the newer properties being of higher value. By the second quarter of the fifteenth century, rents were in decline, and this continued after 1450. At the beginning of the sixteenth century those of the vicars-choral showed a slight increase, but this was short-lived, and after the first decade there was yet a further decline (56). A fall in urban rent values can also be seen in Oxford, although the evidence cited is less comprehensive than that for York, and the most drastic fall seems to have come in the second half of the fifteenth century after a period of relative stability. On the other hand, there is evidence in the fifteenth century of town building of both domestic and commercial property, which was clearly a speculative attempt to secure a profit, so there must have been advantages to be gained from this. One has, for example, cottage rows being erected at Winchester apparently by individuals, and shops being built by the city corporation at Exeter and by the abbey at Tewkesbury (90, pp.67–8).

It is hard to generalize safely about prosperity or decay in the late medieval English town, and different historians have interpreted the evidence in widely varying ways. The most forceful arguments for the period being one of economic growth are those put forward by Bridbury, who points rightly to the phenomenal increases paid by certain towns in taxation between 1334 and 1524. The most dramatic of these increases in percentage terms are, not surprisingly, to be found where the earlier payment was small, as at Lavenham, Totnes and Tiverton, but even major centres such as Norwich and Coventry, which had been assessed at quite a high level in 1334, showed a percentage increase above the national average. On the other hand, there were towns where the increase was small, such as York, Lincoln and Bristol, or even non-existent such as Boston (61, pp.112–13). The most recent writers on the subject have been more cautious, and have pointed out that not all towns can be fitted into the same pattern, and that local factors bulked large in each case (71; 75, p.45). While many of the towns which prospered grew on their manufacture of textiles, York, which had been a cloth town at an earlier date, had been affected by the shift of manufacturing to the West Riding, as well as by the decline of Hull as an export centre. It is also worth remembering that an increased assessment does not necessarily reflect prosperity; there is evidence of considerable urban decay, for example, at Coventry, despite the town's greater tax liability. On balance, Bridbury's more optimistic view seems hard to sustain (75, p.65).

A commonly cited piece of evidence for urban decline is the number of petitions to the Crown for relief from taxation, and equally common is the view of historians that these must be regarded with caution, as the towns were liable to paint their poverty in lurid terms, and to emulate each other in their appeals. The petitions on their own may be unreliable, but the response of the Crown to them must surely be an indication that they had some substance: a government which was regularly short of funds would be unlikely to grant remissions, and the fact that different towns were allowed varying amounts of tax allowance suggests that some attempt was made to calculate the resources available. Lincoln, which on several occasions was totally exempted from paying, seems to have been one of the worst affected (71; 77, pp.272–3).

Bridbury also suggests, from the admissions to the freedom of the boroughs, that the ranks of the citizens were being widened, and that even at a time when rural conditions provided more incentive for men to remain in the country than at an earlier date the towns were still able to attract them (61, pp.62–4 (Tables, 65–9)). The increased number of freemen need not, however, be explained by the greater attractions of town life. Dobson argues convincingly that as the admission of freemen was controlled by the borough authorities, it is more probably that the increased number of admissions was prompted by their desire to spread the load of civic obligations, and to secure money from the payments made on entry to assist shaky borough finances. Citizenship presumably had certain advantages which made it worth a man's while taking it up, but in a period of increasing civic oligarchy one may wonder how greatly these outweighed the disadvantages. Also, although there were marked fluctuations in the number of admissions from year to year, it is clear that from about 1490 the numbers of those admitted at York were consistently lower than they had been from the mid 1380s to the 1440s. There was a trough in the number admitted in the third quarter of the fifteenth century, and a rise in the 1480s was short-lived (70; 71).

One last problem remains, but is probably unanswerable. Is it possible to see private affluence co-existing with corporate poverty? Was it the towns which were poor rather than the townsmen? As far as the urban working class was concerned they may well have been better off in the fifteenth century than they had been previously or were to be later. The evidence of wage-rates, as shown expressed in real terms in the Phelps Brown and Hopkins index, [A.1] points in this direction, and if there was, as seems likely, a decline in urban rent levels, this too could have helped them. It is much harder to say if the ruling merchant employer class was affected adversely, in the same way as its rural counterpart, by the need to pay higher wages, or by a reduction in markets for the commodities which they produced at a time of population decline. Undoubtedly there were men who made substantial fortunes, but there is not sufficient evidence to say whether they were exceptional merely in the scale of their gains or because they contrived to prosper when others failed. The historian must recognize that diversity of fortune existed within towns as well as between them.

It is impossible to summarize the history of English towns in the late Middle Ages in a few convenient generalizations. The variations in their prosperity depended often on how far the developing cloth trade affected individual places; some towns undoubtedly grew, particularly in the early sixteenth century, but they often did so at the expense of others rather than through a serious movement of population from the countryside, although some such drift occurred. Nevertheless, it is likely that in the larger cities at any rate there was considerable change in the personnel of the ruling oligarchies, the members of which clearly were drawn from outside and aspired to return to the country if they could make their fortunes. As yet, there was no well-established 'city interest' to balance the power of the landed class. These oligarchies were, however, powerful and one of the most significant developments in English urban history at this time was the way in which they consolidated their control over town government. They were to continue to dominate it until the nineteenth century.

CHAPTER 7

Industry, trade and shipping

In Chapter 6, it was suggested that one factor which contributed to the variations in fortune between different towns was the extent to which they had been affected by developments in the manufacture of cloth. The growth of this industry was the most fundamental change in the country's economy in the later Middle Ages; where England had previously relied for its exports largely on the export of raw wool for the more advanced industrial economies of the Low Countries and Italy, it became in this period a manufacturing nation in its own right, and cloth replaced wool as its main resource in international trade. The rise in English textile manufacturing was accompanied by changes in its location, and this led to major alterations in the geographical distribution of wealth within the country. Behind these changes lay both developments in the European economy as a whole, and the English exploitation of new manufacturing techniques, from which particular areas benefited more than others.

Taxation of wool exports by the King to finance overseas wars was a further factor which contributed to the growth of the textile industry and of English trade. The imposition of an additional levy on alien exporters in 1303 had led to English merchants playing a major part in handling wool shipments later in the century, but it was Edward III's war taxation for his French campaigns, much of which was derived from levies on wool exports, which did most to promote the development of cloth manufacture in England, by creating a tariff barrier which raised the costs of the raw material to the foreign manufacturers. Although the wool producers seem to have borne part of the tax costs, the substantial increase in cloth production during the war is most easily explicable if a large part of the wool tax was passed on by the exporters to the foreign buyers, while the English cloth manufacturers were able to undercut their Continental rivals (88, pp.39–40). Possibly the direct effects of war on the Flemish cloth towns, which suffered from the campaigns, may have been a further benefit to English producers; indeed this may have been a more important factor in the decline of Flanders than the tariff protection enjoyed by England, because the Dutch cloth industry, which used English wool, also developed at this time at the expense of the Flemish. The extent to which English manufacturers were able to compete in Europe is shown clearly by the extent to which cloth exports increased, even after an export duty was imposed on cloth in 1347, despite the fact that there was no expansion of the market from population growth. The amount shipped abroad continued to rise till the end of the century and remained high until the mid fifteenth century. Despite a fall after the loss of Gascony, exports again increased by the 1470s. By the start of the sixteenth century, cloth had replaced wool as England's main export [A.2]. The clothiers may well have been able to obtain their raw material relatively cheap, because there is some evidence of wool prices being forced down occasionally by over-production, when growers were unable to dispose of the whole annual clip (84, p.312). As most recorded cases of this antedate the main period of enclosures in the mid fifteenth century, it is not clear if the conversion of land from arable to grazing in the period of population decline contributed to this.

Technical progress in the industry lay above all in the increased exploitation of water power. Water-powered fulling mills were not new; indeed they go back at least as far as the thirteenth century. They did, however, give England an advantage over Flanders, where windmills were more common than water-mills. Also driven by water was the 'gig-mill', used for teasing woven cloth by means of teasels secured to rollers. These raised the nap on the cloth, which could then be cropped with shears to give it a smoother finish. The main area for the manufacture of fine broadcloths was the southern Cotswolds, notably in the Stroud valley, where there was not only a supply of high-quality local wool – Cotswold wool was generally regarded as the best in England – but also quantities of fuller's earth and available water power (65, pp.153–6; 84, p.309). Other areas, such as East Anglia and Yorkshire, seem to have concentrated on rather lighter fabrics, worsteds or the narrower cloths called kerseys, and provided rivalry for the Cotswold producers. In many of the cloth-producing areas there were clear signs of prosperity, not least some of the buildings which survive from the period, notably churches such as those at Fairford in Gloucestershire or Long Melford in Suffolk.

The rise of the cloth industry considerably changed the economic geography of England, with new areas emerging to prominence as the result of industrial growth. In the late Middle Ages the West Riding of Yorkshire, particularly the Leeds–Bradford area, emerged as a major centre of the woollen textile industry, as it was to remain, overtaking York as the major centre of the cloth trade in the North (82, p.152). In the South-west, Exeter became a major centre of cloth exports from the 1490s, and by the early sixteenth century some of the smaller Devon towns were also active in the trade, this perhaps contributing to the later growth of West Country shipping activity. Wealthiest of all the centres of cloth manufacturing was East Anglia, particularly Suffolk. The richest town in the area was Lavenham, where trade developed early, and where perhaps three-quarters of the population depended directly or indirectly on cloth manufacturing. For three generations the Spring family played a dominant part in this, and when Thomas Spring III died in 1523 he was wealthier than many of the nobility and was the richest commoner in England outside London; he owned 26 manors in eastern England and held property in 130 parishes (82, pp.13, 94, 152–3). The overseas trade in cloth also contributed to the growing dominance of London, because exports were largely in the hands of the Merchant Adventurers' Company, which was increasingly dominated by the London Mercers' Company (64).

Undoubtedly the cloth industry was the most famous in late medieval England, but one should remember that its importance may have been exaggerated by its being *par excellence* an export industry, and, because its products paid dues on export, being better documented than those which met domestic requirements. Possibly the coal trade, which exported only a small proportion of its production, may have been more active than one might guess from the customs figures. There were exports, as early as the late fourteenth century, from Newcastle and Durham to places as far as Danzig, although Flanders and the Northern Netherlands were more common destinations. Much of the coal mined, however, may have been consumed domestically, or used for iron-smelting or lime-burning. It is hard to judge the extent of the industry, but later developments, particularly in the sixteenth century, seem to have been firmly based on medieval foundations. In 1508–9, 20 per cent of the value of Newcastle's trade was already in coal, and in the following decade there was a boom in coal exports which compensated for a slump in those of wool. Indeed between 1512 and 1519 some attempts were made to sink new mines, presumably to meet demand, but this expansion was followed by contraction during the general European crisis of 1521–26. The geographical spread of the mining industry is hard to ascertain, for much of it is poorly recorded, but incidental references in both ecclesiastical and secular sources show the existence of mines in Yorkshire, Staffordshire and Wales as well as in the North. Nor can one tell the normal value of a mine, although some must have given considerable yields – Wolsey, as bishop of Durham, let out one at a rent of £180 a year (82, pp.164–5).

Possibly the building industry was one of the most substantial in the country, but as it was based on small local units it is virtually impossible to study. Other forms of industry were comparatively small scale. There was some manufacture of salt, both on the east coast and at inland brine springs, but this was insufficient to meet the country's requirements, and substantial supplies had to be imported. The home product tended to be finer in quality than the imported. There is some evidence that Cornish tin-mining maintained a reasonable level of production, although with some fluctuations: a sharp drop just after the Black Death and a boom at the end of the fourteenth century were followed by a period of depression in the half-century after 1430, with a considerable recovery by the early sixteenth century. This last was perhaps due to the development of shaft-mining in addition to open-cast workings (61, pp.25–6; 76, pp.288–9; 82, pp.165–7). There are some references to other forms of metal-working in the country; most notably in the early sixteenth century the areas around Dudley and Birmingham in the Midlands, were becoming centres of ironwork, and there were further developments in such manufacturing at Sheffield where its history goes back further. Admittedly, this was still a minor part of the local economy, compared with, say, leather-working in Birmingham, but the development was to lay the foundation for later generations (82, pp.169, 173).

As noted earlier, internal trade is harder to document than external, but surviving evidence shows its variety. Southampton has some of the best records; its brokage books record tolls paid by merchants or carters entering or leaving the city. It served both as a centre of local trade for its own hinterland, and as a distribution centre for longer-distance trade. The town itself never seems to have developed much industry, but was primarily a place of exchange, from which imported goods were distributed throughout the country and export commodities sent abroad. It obtained foodstuffs from the surrounding countryside, and supplied imported fish, wine and salt in return. Much of the long-distance trade was in commodities connected with the cloth industry, notably dyestuffs such as woad and alum. It was a centre for trade going to Salisbury, the main distribution point for the Wiltshire woollen industry, and sent some goods as far as Coventry, which was famous for its woad-dyed blue cloths. In 1456 Coventry negotiated freedom from tolls in Southampton, as it had already done with another port which served it, namely Bristol. Southampton developed a considerable carting trade, possibly because neither of its rivers, the Itchen and the Test, provided scope for water-borne traffic.

The rivers indeed carried much of England's internal trade. The Severn in the West, and the Thames, the Trent, the Great Ouse and its tributaries, and the Yorkshire Ouse in the East, were undoubtedly major arteries of transport for bulk cargoes. It is noteworthy that the line of the Great North Road runs near where many of these rivers ceased to be navigable, and many towns on the road may have grown up as places where goods were transferred from water freight to carts or pack animals (82, pp.194–200). Water freight also embraced coastal shipping, particularly for heavy loads, such as the coal which was sent from the Tyne to the Thames.

Evidence for road transport is hard to come by, but it is worth remembering that the fifteenth century saw a considerable amount of bridge-building; old timber structures were replaced by stone ones, some of which still survive. It is worth noting that one source of funds for such building came from indulgences, which bishops granted for the purpose, and that another was bequests in wills, although the proportion of testators leaving money to this charity seems to have declined between 1400 and 1530 (82, pp.205–6; 242). When one recollects that bequests were made in the hope of securing the prayers of beneficiaries for the donor's soul, it may be assumed that bridges, and also roads, were in sufficient use for such gifts to be regarded as a good piece of spiritual investment.

When one turns from internal to external trade, one sees that some men at any rate recognized how important it was for England to control the sea. In the verse tract of the late 1430s, the *Libelle of Englyshe Polycye*, the anonymous author, whose sense of politics and economics was more evident than his talent for poetry, taking the design of the gold noble as his symbol, wrote:

> For iiij thynges oure noble sheueth to me,
> Kynge, shype, and swerde, and pouer of the see. (ll. 34–5)

Towards the end too, there is a long exhortation of the need to keep the sea, as the means of protecting England. The author showed shrewd perception of the powers which could be exercised by commercial blockade or by boycott, and he specifically indicates wool and tin as English products which were necessary to the Flemings, who could be brought under pressure by a withdrawal of supplies. Indeed it was the Flemings who were the main target of his attack, far more than England's older French enemies (43, pp.3–6, 15, 53–5). One suspects that this may have been due to a sense of betrayal, when Duke Philip of Burgundy's change of policy in the mid 1430s turned Flanders into a hostile country instead of an ally, and partly to the closeness of past commercial ties, when the wool trade had linked the two lands in any uneasy partnership.

External trade is better documented than internal. The material from the enrolled customs accounts provides, if not entirely reliable evidence, at least a good indication of changes in England's exports. The records of wool and cloth exported, collected by Carus-Wilson and Coleman [A.2, A.3], are an invaluable source, which should continue to yield information on a wide range of subjects. Absolute precision is impossible: there are gaps in the series of accounts from some ports, either because the records have been lost or because the customs had been farmed to the collector for a fixed sum, and there are also some irregularities in the accounting periods, although the customs year normally ran from Michaelmas to Michaelmas. Possibly goods may have been smuggled out without paying duty, although this last should not be exaggerated, because there is no reason to believe that the level of smuggling varied markedly from one period to another, and because with bulk commodities the possible gains were small and the risk of penalties was high (66, pp.21–5). The figures do afford some comparability between years, and even a brief examination of them shows the great shift from wool to cloth as England's main export commodity. This long-term change was far more striking than short-term cyclical variations brought about by political tensions or fluctuations in the general level of economic activity.

Space does not allow more than a cursory examination of the evidence, but one can illustrate its value, and the problems of using it, by looking at the question of how the balance of England's exports changed. By taking four years within our period, each half a century apart, one sees them glaringly clearly. In 1374–75, wool exports paying custom amounted to 27,637 sacks, in 1424–25 12,232 sacks, in 1474–75 8,867 sacks and in 1524–25, 3,432 sacks. Cloth exports for 1374–75 cannot be measured, as the custom on cloth for that year was farmed for all ports except London, and there are considerable gaps in the accounts for adjacent years. (In 1364–65 and 1384–85, years for which there are good sets of figures, the numbers of broadcloths exported are respectively 14,724 and 30,479.) In 1424–25 the figure was 48,368 broadcloths, in 1474–75 31,171 and in 1524–25 96,231. Clearly the cloth figures fluctuate more markedly than those for wool, although those for 1474–75 may have been artifically depressed by the absence of returns from Bristol and Newcastle. The general indication of growth is best shown by the graph compiled from the statistics of the whole period (66) [A.2]. Perhaps the most striking indication of how cloth overtook wool as the country's major export is an action of Henry VII in 1493: in order to apply economic sanctions to the Low Countries, he banned cloth exports, but not those of wool (84, p.283).

Another development clearly reflected in the customs records is the increasing dominance of London, particularly in cloth exports. In 1424–25 its share of these was just over 46 per cent of the national total, in 1474–75 (though perhaps exaggerated by the absence of the Bristol and Newcastle returns) nearly 72 per cent and in 1524–25 81.75 per cent. Its share of wool exports rose too, though less strikingly, in 1374–75 and 1424–25 the figure was between 40 and 45 per cent, by 1474–75 it exceeded 50 per cent and in 1524–25 it was 66 per cent. It is likely, particularly if one allows for the gaps in the 1474–75 returns, that the period when London secured its massive commercial lead over the rest of the country was the last quarter of the fifteenth and the first quarter of the sixteenth century. At the turn of the century, in 1499–1500, the figures (although marred by the absence of any from Southampton) show London's share of cloth exports as 68 per cent and of wool as just over 70 per cent (66, pp.77, 111).

London was also becoming dominant in other spheres of trade. By the end of the fourteenth century, the London skinners had control of the import of skins for the fur trade, and provincial merchants had been squeezed out. The records of salt imports are incomplete, and the only tables which can be compiled have to draw on several years in any period to include all the ports involved. This does not allow sufficiently for annual variations for the figures to permit strict statistical analysis, but even with these the changes are too striking to be totally ignored. In the late fourteenth century three ports, London, Exeter and Yarmouth, imported similar quantities, each taking between 13.5 per cent and 15 per cent of the national total. London's share in the mid fifteenth century was similar, but it had been overtaken by Yarmouth and Bristol, with 41.5 per cent and 19 per cent respectively. However, by the latter years of the century, both Yarmouth and Bristol had declined, and London was taking over 71 per cent of the imports.

The capital's importance in the cloth trade is seen in the part played in it by the Fellowship of the Merchant Adventurers of London. The term 'merchant adventurer' was originally applied to any merchant trading in cloth overseas; there were groups of them from various towns including Newcastle and York, and others were drawn from several of the London companies, but gradually the term was limited to a group within the Mercers. Again, originally groups of 'adventurers' were recognized in trade with various lands – one trading with Prussia secured royal recognition in 1391, another with the Netherlands in 1407 and a third with the Scandinavian lands in 1408, but eventually the Netherlands group secured for itself the specific name of the Merchant Adventurers' Company (64, pp.143–50). The company's corporate organization became tighter in the fifteenth century, particularly in the latter half of it; this culminated in 1486 with the formal recognition of the Fellowship of the Merchant Adventurers of London. From the late 1470s pressure had been put on merchants outside London to join the company there, and after some resistance they had to yield (64, pp.153–60, 172–6). The company imposed regulations on its members, but individuals still traded on their own account.

The organization of wool exports was more tightly controlled. The needs of war taxation in the fourteenth century, and the contribution which the custom on wool made to this, had led to the growth of a system whereby sales of wool had to be made through a staple town, sometimes in England and sometimes abroad. By the beginning of the fifteenth century the wool Staple was fixed at Calais, where it remained. The Staplers did not acquire a complete monopoly; merchants from the northern counties were able to export direct to the Netherlands and, more important, Italian merchants could secure licences to export wool either by land or by sea through the Straits of Gibraltar (94, pp.43–7).

The problem of keeping Calais garrisoned and of paying the troops there was closely linked with the siting of the Staple and the relations between the government and the merchants. On a number of occasions the soldiers of the garrison seized wool supplies in the town when their wages were in arrears; in 1407 they sold the wool and in 1421 the Staplers had to pay £4,000 to recover it. In the mid century too, in 1448 and 1454, the garrison again gave trouble (84, pp.258, 271, 275). In practice, money from wool taxation was the main source of funds for the garrison, and this raised problems as wool exports declined. From 1466 the company took over the financial management of the garrison, with the mayor of the Staple becoming *de facto* royal treasurer of the town. This agreement was renewed four times, the last in 1515, but eventually the company had to be released from its responsibility on grounds of poverty. It had probably been the wish to secure ready cash to pay the troops that was responsible for legislation in 1429 requiring that the entire price of the wool must be paid in gold and silver, and that one-third of the price, in bullion, be handed over to the Calais mint (84, pp.261, 275, 279–80). Political and financial considerations were probably responsible for keeping the Staple at Calais; in strictly economic terms it might have been more advantageous if it had been moved closer to the rising Dutch cloth towns.

Inside the company there were tensions, and in 1429, along with the bullion legislation, an attempt was made to change the form of trading. Instead of merchants dealing individually with clients, all wool was to be graded and pooled according to its quality, and profits were to be divided in accordance with the quantity that each had brought to the Staple. The men behind this ordinance seem to have been the greater merchants, who hoped to control the trade more strictly in their own interests, but the new system was never wholly enforced. Merchants were able to secure exemption from it, and although it is not clear who emerged more strongly from disputes in the 1440s, by the 1450s control of the Staple seems to have passed to men hostile to it (84, pp.261, 270–1, 273).

One last aspect of English trade must be considered, namely the state of the shipping industry. Our knowledge of this is patchy, and it is certain that the quantity of trade is not a precise reflection of the prosperity of English shipping, as many exports were carried in foreign vessels. The Italian wool trade, in particular, was largely carried in Venetian and Florentine galleys until the middle of the fifteenth century. Florentine shipping then declined, and the galley fleet is last recorded at Southampton in 1478. Thereafter, although the Florentines continued to import English wool, they did not carry it in their own ships, and in the 1480s proposals were made for a wool staple at Pisa, with English ships having the monopoly of the carrying. A treaty was agreed in 1490, although a concession was made to the Venetians to exempt them from the Staple. The value of the treaty, however, was short-lived, because of the disruptions of the Italian wars, and more particularly the revolt of Pisa from Florence in 1494. There is also a record of a Spanish ship carrying cloth out of Bristol in the 1460s, and it may not have been untypical, although undoubtedly English vessels were engaged in the Iberian trade. Henry VII had two Navigation Acts passed, in 1486 and 1489, but their scope was narrow, being concerned primarily with the Gascon trade, and no general attempt was made to develop English mercantile shipping (110, p.220).

The early pilot books give a fair indication of the scope of English nautical activity. They give information on the east coast of England, the English Channel and the western seaboard, including Ireland. They also contain information about the sea routes round Brittany, and south to Gascony and the Iberian peninsula, although they are markedly fuller north of Bordeaux (63, pp.24–6). They do not cover the Mediterranean, where England does not appear to have played a substantial part in trade until at least after the accession of the Tudors. There had been some earlier pioneers, notably Robert Sturmy of Bristol, who sent two ill-fated ventures there in 1446 and 1457, the first ending in the wreck of his ship off Greece and the second in a spoliation by the Genoese, which provoked retaliation against the Genoese in England and the seizure of their goods. A surviving volume of pursers's accounts shows another Bristol ship going to Oran in 1480–1 (94, pp.226–9; 100).

In the early 1480s there are some indications that English seamen were seeking to extend their activities. Portuguese protests seem to have crushed an attempt by two Englishmen, possibly with Spanish support, to secure a foothold in the Guinea trade, and around the same time, in 1480 and 1481, Bristol ships were exploring out into the Atlantic in search of the 'Isle of Brasil' (45, pp.19–23, 187–9). The available information on these voyages is sparse and the aims of the voyagers unknown, but it is possible that there was a regular series of them. It is not clear if they were being tempted to the south in search of sugar or if the Atlantic voyages were mainly concerned with fishing. Bristol had previously been heavily involved in the Iceland trade, but had been coming under pressure from increasing Hanse power there, and its merchants may well have been looking for alternative supplies of fish – it is worth stressing that the ships sent out in 1481 in search of the 'Isle of Brasil' were carrying a large quantity of salt (45, pp.188–9; 94, pp.177–82). The 'Isle of Brasil' was mythical, but fifteenth-century Atlantic charts suggest that belief in lands across the ocean was not uncommon, and there is more than just possibility that the Bristol men had heard of some landfall in them before 1480, perhaps when ships had been blown off course by abnormal wind conditions. Is it just a curious coincidence that one of the Bristol ships involved in the exploration of 1481 had on its previous voyage called at the Franciscan convent at Huelva, where Columbus was later to secure support for his proposed voyages?

The culmination of these explorations was John Cabot's discovery of Newfoundland in 1497, an event which contemporaries clearly recognized as a major achievement. Henry VII, despite his notorious parsimony, gave rewards to those who went to the new lands, and voyages continued, at least sporadically, until the end of his reign. The reaction to the discovery, that it would mean that there would be no need of the Icelandic fishing grounds in future, makes it fairly certain that even if there had been accidental sightings of the New World before that date, no systematic attempts had been made to explore it further nor to exploit the resources of the Newfoundland Banks (45, pp.214–16).

Why did England fail to exploit the discovery? No doubt Henry VIII's desire for military glory in Europe played a part; the payment of rewards recorded in the Household Books cease with his accession. It may also be that the early returns from the voyages proved small, and that it was felt that investment in them did not provide an adequate reward for those involved. Bristol, too, was in decline, losing some of its old trade to Southampton and Exeter, so its merchants could have had less to invest in this enterprise. Not until the second half of the sixteenth century, when there was a desire to combat Spanish power and to tap the resources of the Indies, did an English enterprise to North America again become attractive. Because of this delay in time, it is perhaps an exaggeration to say that the expansion of English maritime activity between 1460 and 1520 prepared the way for seizing opportunities which were opening up in many parts of the world (63, p.163).

The expansion of English shipping, however, certainly occurred. While in the fifteenth century it was rare to designate a man by the title 'shipowner', this occupation became commoner in the sixteenth (100). Some parts of the country showed more significant growth than others: on the east coast, the number of sailings not only rose in absolute terms between the 1460s and the early sixteenth century, but the proportion of those by English ships approximately doubled, although there were some exports which were largely carried in foreign vessels. In the Channel the Cinque Ports were to decline, but there was considerable growth in the West Country, between Southampton and Plymouth. In Devon and Cornwall indeed there seems to have been a long tradition of piratical and privateering activity in addition to legitimate trade, which may well have laid the foundation for the activities of seamen from this part of the country in the Elizabethan age (63, pp.159–60).

In conclusion, the main areas of growth in English trade and industry were probably in cloth and shipping, although one must always allow for the possibility that some less well-documented sectors of the economy were also making significant advances. With the growth in industry there was also a significant development of trade, particularly in the early Tudor period, and with it came the increasing dominance of London in the English economy. It was not itself a centre of manufacturing, but it outstripped all other ports as a point of transit for English exports and became thereby a major entrepôt of international trade. London merchants were able to assert their authority over their provincial rivals, and with this one can see the beginnings of centralization in the economy.

CHAPTER 8

War: profit and loss

For the first half of the period covered in this book, and again towards its end, England was involved in foreign wars. For a considerable part of the intervening period there was recurrent civil strife between magnate and dynastic factions. How far did war affect the economy or bring about social change? It had different results for various sections in the community, but all were affected by it in some way, either directly or indirectly. The military classes, the lords and the gentry, were directly involved in the wars as participants, but as landowners they also had an indirect concern, because trading changes resulting from war affected the profits of their estates. As a social group they could record both gains and losses from war, and there has been some debate among historians about how far a balance sheet can be struck for the country as a whole, whether England gained or lost from its military operations. The trading community could suffer from the hazards which war created for shipping or through the destruction of possible export markets. As we saw in Chapter 7, furthermore, the domestic cloth industry developed during the period under the tariff protection of royal taxation and as a result of war damage to existing European textile centres.

Clearly, civil war was more likely than overseas campaigns to have an immediate effect on men's lives. For members of the nobility the struggles of Lancaster and York could have drastic results, particularly for those who incurred forfeiture through ending up on the losing side; although attainders could be reversed and lands restored, this might take a long time (130, Ch.5). It is harder to measure how far the campaigns of the civil wars affected the great mass of the population or the country's internal economy, but the damage may not have been particularly great, as much of the fighting was confined to limited areas. Although the passage of an army could alarm civilians in its path, there is little evidence for mass devastations. Indeed the endemic disorder of medieval society, which was little different in the late Middle Ages from what it had been earlier, may have caused as much economic disruption in a locality such as the East Anglia of the Pastons. How far East Anglia was typical is hard to say, and the historian must guard against making generalizations from evidence which is geographically limited: certainly the Stonor correspondence suggests that Oxfordshire suffered less from the kind of violence recorded in the Paston Letters (17; 24).

England's external wars were fought principally in France, so most Englishmen had little direct experience of warfare, apart from those in the North, where relations with Scotland were always likely to break out into open hostility. However, full-scale campaigns in the northern counties were rare, and the real problem there was one of pillaging raids. This was exacerbated by the general unruliness of society, which was perhaps more deep-seated than further south, and although the emergence of the Neville and Percy families to a position of dominance in the region provided some barrier to external threats, their mutual rivalry was detrimental to local order and a potential threat to the economy of the area. Feuds lower in the social scale, such as that between the Heron and Manners families from 1428 to 1431, where both parties could count on influential support from greater men, could prove hard to solve and necessitate impartial arbitration from outside (209, pp.197–201). Despite the problems of both Scottish raids and internal disorder, the coal industry of Northumberland and Durham was able to make substantial developments, with Newcastle as the centre of exports (Ch.7; 82, pp.164–5).

England's involvement in European wars fell into two broad periods, separated by over half a century. The first ended when Gascony fell to the French in 1453, and the second began when the ambitions of Henry VIII for military glory drew the country into the conflicts of a Europe which had been greatly changed by the emergence of powerful new states in the last quarter of the fifteenth century. In the intervening years only one major English army crossed to France, in 1475, when Edward IV let himself be bought off by a treaty and substantial cash payments. Politically, relations remained tense for much of this middle period, sufficiently so to affect economic links between England and France, and England was allied with the semi-independent feudatories of the French Crown, Burgundy and Brittany, on a number of occasions until they were absorbed into the lands of the Valois dynasty in 1477 and 1492 respectively. The Burgundian alliance was closely connected with English economic interests, because the Low Countries, which were the most economically advanced section of the Burgundian duchy, were major trading partners of England, particularly as a market for exports of raw wool. This was recognized in the 1430s by the author of *The Libelle of Englyshe Polycye*, when he advocated the use of a trade embargo to force Flemish compliance with English policies (43, pp.5–6). Another overseas power with which England had uneasy relations, particularly over trading matters, was the league of Hanse towns of North Germany; there were times when these developed into open warfare, but although this affected trade, it did not have the same repercussions on society as did the wars with France.

Political ties between England and Gascony in the years before 1453 also had economic implications, because although the two had originally been linked by dynastic chance, their economies could complement each other. Gascony had developed a specialized economy dominated by viticulture, with some production of woad and iron, but its corn production was inadequate to meet its full needs. Originally England could supply the necessary quantities of corn from its own surplus, and later it was able to re-export corn from the Baltic, which was one of the major granaries for the lands of western Europe in the late Middle Ages. Gascony also provided an outlet for English cloth exports.

One effect of these trading links was that prices of wine in England were directly linked with the state of the war in South-west France. When the war was renewed in the 1370s, the price of wine in London rose to 10d. per gallon, although during the truce of 1375–77 it fell again to 6d. It was not held at this level; for most of the 1390s it was 8d. and dropped to 6d. again only in 1398. For the first half of the fifteenth century, Gascony was under less pressure, probably because Henry V's campaigns had shifted the bulk of military activity to northern France, but even so war had a serious effect on wine exports. These reached a peak during the truce of 1444–49, but were halved when war was renewed in the latter year. However, even political hostility did not entirely break these old economic links. In 1455 Charles VII of France forbade the grant of safe-conducts to the English, but this ban was relaxed and trade, albeit reduced in volume, continued until 1462. A truce in the following year did much to restore the old trade, and the Treaty of Picquigny of 1475 eased many of the restrictions which had been imposed on it (64, Ch.7; 93; 94, pp.212–13).

It is hard to judge how far and in what ways these fluctuations in the wine trade affected the population as a whole. Drinkers of wine, who would be affected by price changes, were a minority, as most Englishmen drank ale, the supply and cost of which would depend on the latest harvest. The most serious effects were probably felt by the men involved in the Gascon shipping trade, as this declined to match the reduced volume of commodities on the move. The port principally connected with this was Bristol, and it may have been the existence of surplus tonnage that led its seamen to turn their attention to new ventures in the fifteenth century, including both attempts to penetrate the Mediterranean trade and the later voyages into the Atlantic. The reduced value of trade was not confined to imports; the fall in these was parallelled, although not precisely, by a decline in cloth exports, which was particularly marked at Bristol. The customs accounts there for the decade 1450–60 show that the average annual export of broadcloths, by both denizens and aliens, was a third lower than it had been in the years 1440–50 (94, pp.334–5).[1] Wine imports over the same period were reduced by just over 40 per cent.

It is clear, therefore, that the effects of the French War on the Gascon trade were a major factor in the fortunes of Bristol; in London matters were rather different. One cannot compare exactly the customs accounts from the two ports, because those for London ending in 1460 conclude at the end of July instead of the normal date of Michaelmas, so the second period employed in the comparison is that of the eleven years 1450–61. Imports of wine suffered a similar drop to those at Bristol; indeed the average annual import fell even more drastically, by over 45 per cent, but the decline in cloth exports, by only a little over 15 per cent, was much less. The contrast is even more marked when one examines the exports in detail; those by denizens fell by only 2 per cent, those by Hansard merchants actually rose by over 6 per cent, while those by other aliens fell by over 77 per cent. Represented as a share of the market, this means that denizens increased their figure from 43.0 per cent to 49.7 per cent, the Hansards theirs from 35.6 per cent to 44.5 per cent, while other aliens, whose earlier share had been a substantial 21.4 per cent now had only 5.8 per cent (94, pp.345–6). It is not clear who these other aliens were – some were probably Italians – but it is probable that a substantial proportion of them were engaged in trade with Gascony or other French lands. On this occasion the Hansards seem to have been the main beneficiaries from the decline in the activity of other alien merchants, but they too could be affected by political rivalry, and periods of tension between England

and the Hanse towns, even if this fell short of war, were marked by substantial falls in cloth exports by the Hanse merchants. The year 1475 was to prove crucial for the recovery of cloth exports, as the Treaty of Utrecht with the Hanse and the Treaty of Picquigny with France did much to restore the level of exports in the latter years of Edward IV's reign (94, pp.26–9, 34–6). From this date onwards to the reign of Henry VIII, the trend of exports continued to rise, although there were some years when one can see a temporary decline [A.3].

The manufacture of cloth itself had of course been considerably affected by war. As we saw earlier (Ch.7), wool taxation to raise war funds had provided a protective tariff for the textile industry, and the war had damaged one of the main Continental cloth-manufacturing centres in Flanders. The effects of war, however, could also prove potentially damaging in a new way as England became more closely involved with the wider economy in western Europe; a slump in exports, even if this were due to factors outside English control, could lead to domestic unemployment, and in the 1520s complaints were made about this in the textile areas of Suffolk (Ch.4). It is probably fair to say that although some aspects of the economy were stimulated by war, for most merchants it was primarily a source of problems.

While war could create serious difficulties for the merchant class, other social groups looked at it in a different light. The values of the ruling class were essentially military, and war was not incidental to life so much as its *raison d'être*. The cult of chivalry, however artificial some aspects of it were, was one in which men really believed, and this undoubtedly contributed to a glorification of the horrors of war. The fourteenth-century French canonist Honoré Bouvet, whose *Tree of Battles* was widely circulated in various languages as well as in the original French, held that a man could engage in war on either side without imperilling his soul, and that if the combatant believed the war to be just, he might justly engage in it. Besides being a way of life, with a related set of moral values, war also had a strongly material side for the noble class, and could provide an income as well as an occupation. Some ways in which the nobility profited from war were more acceptable to the *mores* of the age than others, some more or less guaranteed reward, while others gave opportunity to gamble for high profits. Irrespective of a man's rank, it was not thought below his dignity to receive payments from the King for military service, and the wages payable varied with the rank of the individual. This remuneration was payable whether or not the war was successful. A less legitimate gain, but one which might still be made in an unsuccessful war, was to exploit the system of contracting to provide troops. A captain could economize on the equipping and provisioning of his men, or continue to draw pay for men who had died or deserted. A successful war provided other gains. Englishmen undoubtedly benefited from the fact that the great war was fought mainly on French soil, where they could loot at will, and during periods of victory successful captains were rewarded with offices in conquered territories, such as custodianships of castles, or with grants of land. Finally, and most risky, there was the possibility of ransoms. This was a gambler's reward, because the chance of war might leave a man as either the recipient or the payer of a large sum. Success could raise a man from comparative insignificance to wealth and fame, but capture could cripple an estate with the burden of payment.

The most conspicuous financial gains by English combatants were made in the earlier phase of the Anglo-French wars or in the wars with Scotland – the esquire John Coupland, who captured David II of Scotland in 1346, received lands worth £500 a year and the status of banneret, and many in the English army at Poitiers in 1356 received rich rewards (88, p.30). In the later English victories too, many men made profits. When the war went badly, however, there were corresponding losses. Robert Moleyns, Lord Hungerford, captured at Castillon in 1453, was valued for ransom at £6,000, a sum inflated to almost £10,000 by the cost of his maintenance while a prisoner till his release in 1459 and by the charges of the merchants who negotiated the exchange of the money. The family lands were mortgaged to meet the payments, and worse was to follow. Robert's loyalty to Margaret of Anjou and the Lancastrians led to attainder and forfeiture, which in turn compelled his mother to sell two manors of her own to meet the demands of creditors from whom the ransom money had been borrowed (88, pp.29–32, 126–7).

Profit and loss from war was not necessarily always a matter of individual enterprise. The relationship of brotherhood in arms among men of the military class involved support in such material matters as well as in battle and social action. It could be enforced by law, and a sworn companion could claim a right to the gains of war made by a dead partner. Similarly, if one companion were captured, his partner was under an obligation to contribute to his ransom. The best illustration of what the relationship involved is found in the careers of two esquires, Nicholas Molyneux and John Winter. In 1421 they entered a contract to be loyal to each other without dissimulation or fraud. This provided for arrangements to secure ransom money if necessary, to pool any gains of war and invest them profitably, and, if one left a widow, to make some provision for her and give some protection for surviving children. Both men were of obscure origin, but by the late 1420s they entered the service of Sir John Fastolf; by 1433 Moly-neux was the latter's receiver-general, as well as serving the regent, Bedford. In the 1440s, by which time Winter had died, Molyneux entered the service of Rich-ard, duke of York. In Winter's will, he seems to have disregarded the terms of the original partnership, for Molyneux became involved in litigation against two of the feoffees under it, and the eventual settlement suggests that his claim was justified. It should be stressed that even when the war was going badly for Eng-land, the partnership secured profits, which remained in England, even although the gains ultimately passed to other hands than those of the partners.

This point should be emphasized, because there has been debate among his-torians, particularly between M. M. Postan and K. B. McFarlane, about how far the war affected the total wealth of England. Postan's view was gloomy – war destroyed wealth and England grew poorer. Within the country, he argued, war transferred wealth from one group to another, and although war taxation pro-duced a class of native financiers, as for example William de le Pole, for the first time in English history, it did not change the structure of the national economy. Wealth went on a circular tour, and royal taxation was either wasted or enriched a class of profiteers, either the war captains or the purveyors who operated between the Exchequer and the army. Wealth, originally derived from the land, returned to the purchase of land, and there was no marked constructive investment of capital. Certainly much of this is true; war led to a redistribution of wealth, but Postan does not consider whether, if there had been no war, wealth would have been more constructively employed by the land-owning class. One may doubt if it would (91; 92, pp.174–5; 93).[2]

McFarlane argued that on balance England did not lose from the war, and if one thinks in strict cash terms, the evidence supports him. French raids on the English south coast may have inflicted some damage, but in general the wealthier parts of the country were free of fighting. By contrast, war was endemic in France. English raids, even when militarily unsuccessful, provided loot for the attackers, who were sometimes paid to go away, as at St Sauveur in 1375 or Buzançais in 1412. (The buying off of Edward IV's 1475 expedition was in the same tradition.) Victorious campaigns, such as those of Henry V, led to much larger gains. The English in fifteenth-century France were like successful speculators, appropriating the assets of the conquered land, and escaping with their profits before the crash of 1453 (86; 88, pp.31–9). Even while the war was going badly for the English, they suffered fewer major military defeats, and fewer English nobles had to pay ransoms than received payments from their French equivalents. The final withdrawal without major disaster enabled them to preserve some profit. In conclusion one may say that the magnate class, and particularly the military captains, were the main beneficiaries, but that the gains of war were often fortuitous and certainly unevenly spread.

McFarlane's study of the investment of Sir John Fastolf's profits of war is the best illustration of how an individual could emerge successfully from a war which had gone badly. In 1445, his English estates had an annual value of over £1,061, and about three-quarters of this came from estates purchased out of his war gains. His inherited lands were negligible and the bulk of the balance was represented by his acquisitions through marriage. The landed purchases had cost £13,855 and some 90 per cent of them had been made after 1420. Fastolf's methods in securing gains are shown by an episode recorded in the archives of the Parlement of Paris. In 1423, the regent, Bedford, had released an important prisoner of Fastolf's, Guillaume Remon, in return for the submission of Compiègne. Fastolf sought, and obtained, compensation for this, admittedly ten years later, and also claimed a right to the ransoms of various merchants whom he had freed from Remon. His right to these was admitted – only the scale of payment was disputed. After 1445 Fastolf continued to buy property – indeed his best-known purchase, the Boar's Head Inn in Southwark, was bought for £200 in 1450. Despite some losses in the final débâcle in France, he was able to salvage something by selling lands unprofitably before the end (87).[3]

Fastolf was not unique. The Danish-born Sir Andrew Ogard, who served in France and was knighted at the Battle of Verneuil, where incidentally Fastolf was promoted banneret, received letters of denization in 1433 and held offices in France worth £1,000 annually. From these gains he bought the manors of Rye in Hertfordshire and of Emneth, near Wisbech, and indulged in substantial building and repairs there. He kept a chapel with four priests and sixteen choristers at Rye

House, at a cost of £100 a year. Nor was it only such 'new men' who devoted war gains to building. Richard Beauchamp, earl of Warwick, rebuilt the south side of Warwick Castle, enlarged the college at St Mary's Church, Warwick, and built or restored manor houses or castles in five different counties.

Although these examples suggest that the French wars did not impoverish England, clearly the inflow of bullion was not directed into economic developments which increased the country's productive capacity. This is not surprising: the military class was more concerned with conspicuous display than with the creation of national wealth, and it would be anachronistic to expect them to have any other outlook. While lords were concerned about returns from their estates, their normal practice was to exploit traditional resources rather than to seek more profitable areas for investment, even at a time when population decline made it hard for them to find tenants and had reduced rent levels and the income from them. There is, however, one other problem requiring study which could illuminate the question of how profitable the war was. The fact that lands were available for purchase presupposes that there were sellers as well as buyers, and much less is known about who these were, and why they were selling, than is known about the purchasers. A detailed examination of the causes of land sales in the fifteenth century and of the extent to which the inflow of bullion from the spoils of France affected land prices, would be a major contribution to our knowledge of how the war influenced the English economy and society.

The end of the French wars did not mean the end of warfare among Englishmen. The civil disorders and dynastic feuds between Lancaster and York presumably led to some destruction of wealth, although it is virtually impossible to judge how much. Some men certainly lost their estates, although they might recover them later as political fortunes changed, but there is no real reason to believe that the estates themselves were normally impoverished by the fighting. Also, although some families were undoubtedly hard hit by the conflicts, some men were able to avoid political entanglements and concentrate on their private interests, even men from the highest ranks of society such as John de la Pole, duke of Suffolk (148). What we do not know is how far these were typical, but it is worth remembering that the letters of both the Pastons and the Stonors are largely concerned with family concerns rather than national politics. Both families had ties with greater men, who were more concerned with affairs of State, and they were affected by political turmoil, particularly the Stonors, who suffered forfeiture in 1483 for rebelling against Richard III, but both had come through the earlier phase of the dynastic struggle with relatively minor scars.

Whereas there have been arguments over the economic consequences of overseas war in the fourteenth and fifteenth centuries, there is no disagreement that renewed English intervention in Europe in the sixteenth was massively expensive to the nation. Henry VII had been sufficiently discreet to avoid continental entanglements and their resulting expense, but his son was more concerned with illusory glory than with real power. His wars with France between 1511 and 1514 and between 1522 and 1525 brought no economic returns, the occupation of Tournai from 1513 to 1519 involved loss rather than gain and subsidy payments to continental allies involved the export of national resources (82, p.209). After the outbreak of the Reformation crisis, Henry's overseas ambitions were unabated, and it seems certain that their cost played a major part in prompting the rapacious seizure and subsequent disposal of the monastic lands, the greatest tenurial revolution in English history since the Norman Conquest.

The effects of war on the economy must be seen as uneven. It could influence individual fortunes directly as well as having more pervasive consequences for the economy as a whole. As far as the aristocracy were concerned, it did not lead to fundamental changes in the social structure; where wealth changed hands, it was generally within the existing dominant class. The financial difficulties arising out of Henry VIII's wars were, however, to clear the way for a massive redistribution of landed resources through the spoliation of the Church. The greatest changes brought about by war were probably in the development of the cloth industry and the rise of the great clothiers to prominence within the English merchant class. At the same time, one must remember that there were other aspects of the economy which were virtually unaffected by war; one sees this in the growth of the mining interest in the North-east, and most conspicuously in the continuation of trading connections with areas even after the political ties which had created them had been broken. In such cases, the effects of war lasted only as long as the duration of hostilities, and trade was resumed after the restoration of peace.

----

1. By using decades as units of comparison, one in fact underestimates the extent of the drop, which had already begun in the years 1448–50 and figures for these years lower the average for the earlier period from the peak immediately preceding the decline.
2. In Postan's latest work on the subject (92), he rather toned down some of his earlier views.
3. Fastolf's French lands, worth £85 per annum were sold for £847, approximately a rate of ten years' purchase, while the normal cost of lands was about twenty years' purchase. It is a measure of Fastolf's shrewdness that his own acquisitions, at an average of about eighteen years' purchase, cost him rather less than the current market rate for land (87).

PART TWO

The nation of England

CHAPTER 9

England: nation and localities

The study of the English economy in the late Middle Ages shows that there were wide discrepancies of fortune between different parts of the country, and that any attempt to understand its development must take into consideration not only such general factors as population change and the effects of war but also the immediate local factors which determined why one area could outstrip another in prosperity or decline. At the same time, the historian is liable to think in terms of England as a nation, and of English society as essentially one. Is this a valid belief, or should one regard society and politics also as being essentially local in character? It is fair to say, particularly when one is considering overseas relations, that there was some form of national sentiment, but at the same time one should guard against the assumption that this was a dominant force in determining men's attitudes on all occasions.

A self-conscious sense of national identity is a relatively sophisticated idea, and is unlikely to find expression outside a small educated class. It can also exist in a cruder form, whenever a man draws some distinction between himself and the member of another nation, and there is no doubt that such an attitude existed. The early-fourteenth-century chronicler, Geoffrey le Baker, tells of an episode in 1338, during a French raid on Southampton. The townsmen had secured support from the rural hinterland, and a young knight in the invading force was clubbed to the ground by an English rustic. He called for quarter, offering to pay a ransom (*Rançon*), but the peasant retorted, 'Yes, I know you're a Françon', and killed him, not knowing, as Baker says, the other's *idioma* (88, p.19). Baker tells the story partly to show the varying attitudes to war between the knightly and non-knightly classes, but it also shows how men saw in different languages a clear distinction between nations. In the late fourteenth century, one finds Wyclif using the word 'nation' (which was susceptible of a wide variety of usages), to denote men who had been bred in England (132).

Here then were two criteria, language and place of birth, which men of different kinds employed to distinguish between nations. Early in the fifteenth century, the problem of what constituted a nation arose as a practical issue at the Council of Constance, and, as might be expected in an assembly which contained many distinguished academics, the issue was debated in theoretical terms, although the original cause of the debate was essentially political. The organization of the Council, borrowed from that of the universities, was by 'nations' (principally in order to restrict the voting powers of the large number of Italians), but the French objected to the English existing as a separate nation from the Germans – significantly in the Arts Faculty at the University of Paris the English and the Germans were included in the same one. The dispute took place after

the English victory at Agincourt and at a time of growing alliance between Henry
V and the Emperor Sigismund against the French, and there is little doubt that
the principal French spokesman on the subject, Cardinal Pierre d'Ailly, was
largely concerned with cutting the enemy down to size. The argument, however,
forced the English to justify their national identity, and the arguments employed
give some idea of how men thought at the time. England, it was asserted, possessed all the characteristics of an authentic nation:

> whether nation be understood as a people marked off from others by blood rela-
> tionship and habit of unity or by peculiarities of language, the most sure and positive
> sign and essence of a nation in divine and human law . . . or whether nation be
> understood as it should be, as a territory equal to that of the French nation (132).

The English were in fact trying to claim the authentic characteristics of a nation
irrespective of how it was defined, including an attempt to cover English claims
over Scotland and Ireland, despite the absence of any 'habit of unity' in the former case or of a shared language in the latter. It is however significant that blood
relationship and peculiarities of speech, the criteria noted in the last paragraph,
were both mentioned.

The fact that England virtually possessed a common language is also reflected
in the increasing extent to which it was used both by individuals and by corporate
bodies. Within the territory of England proper, the only surviving separate language was Cornish, and it is significant that this linguistic divergence was itself
an issue during political troubles in the mid sixteenth century: one plea which the
Cornish rebels made in 1549 in favour of the traditional liturgy was that 'we the
Cornyshe men (whereof certen of us understande no Englysh) utterly refuse thys
newe Englysh' (73, p.135). But Cornwall was exceptional, and one marked characteristic of the period from the late fourteenth century onwards was the increasing victory of the English tongue. Late in the reign of Edward III, it came into
use as the language of the Convocation of Canterbury, instead of Latin and
French, in 1399 Henry of Lancaster laid claim to the throne in English (22, p.43)
and from 1395 the use of English generally became more common in wills (135,
pp.209–10). In the letters of Henry V, the language was always English, a fact
which was noted by his contemporaries. When the London Brewers' Company
resolved in 1442 to keep its records in English, it justified its decision by the fact
that Henry had preferred the 'common idiom' in his letters (135, pp.117–19).
Again, when the historian considers the available sources for the late Middle
Ages, it is noteworthy that one of the major collections of narratives, the London
City Chronicles, was in the vernacular, although some of the earlier city chroniclers had used Latin or Anglo-Norman. In literature too, the period sees the
increasing use of English, and although some bilingual (or even trilingual) writing
occurs in the fifteenth century, notably in macaronic verse, the major authors,
from Chaucer and Langland through Malory to Skelton and Wyatt, wrote entirely
or principally in English. Admittedly, even at the end of our period, Thomas
More still wrote some major works in Latin, but these were the works of a
humanist scholar thinking of an international audience, and he was also prepared
to produce an English version of the *History of Richard III* and to write his

Confutation of Tyndale in the vernacular. In the fifteenth century Fortescue, too, was a bilingual writer, with the English *Governance of England* and the Latin *De Laudibus Legum Anglie*. The only significant survival of French was in the specialized language of the common law and reflects the conservatism of the legal profession.

The use of English by the intellectual classes shows that it was becoming more socially acceptable, and the assertion that language was a distinguishing criterion of nationhood reveals a growing measure of national self-awareness. Furthermore, and even more important, various writers clearly show that they thought of England as a nation. Two fifteenth-century archbishops of Canterbury, Chichele and Bourchier, write of 'the Church of England' in terms which show that they regarded it as a distinctive entity within the Church Universal, and one in which they could take considerable national pride. Chief Justice Fortescue compared the prosperity of England and the quality of its law with the poverty of France and the arbitary rule of the King there (10, pp.68–9; 30, pp.113–15, 137). The Venetian author of the *Italian Relation of England* commented specifically on the English sense of national pride, and presumably was thinking of attitudes which he encountered generally and not merely the point of view of the more literate: '. . . the English are great lovers of themselves and everything belonging to them; they think that there are no other men than themselves, and no other world but England; and whenever they see a handsome foreigner, they say "he looks like an Englishman" ' (35, pp.20–1). Chronicle writings bear out the validity of this comment, for many of them are strongly patriotic, sometimes, as in the case of the *Gesta Henrici Quinti*, combining patriotism with exhortation: 'Our England (*Anglia nostra*) has reason to rejoice and reason to grieve' (at the victory of Agincourt and at the destruction and death of Christians), 'Let our England be zealous in pleasing God unceasingly.' Lest one might think that such patriotic sentiments came from a court milieu, for the anonymous author was probably a royal chaplain, one should remember that similar sentiments and the attribution of victory to God also occur in the London City Chronicles. Possibly monastic writers may have been slightly less chauvinist in outlook; the St Albans chronicler at least is less effusive about Agincourt, although he too notes the triumphant reception which the King received on his return (16, p.111; 22, p.70; 39, pp.xviii, 98–9).

The culmination of these claims to national identity and of sentiments of this nature came in the preamble to Henry VIII's Act in Restraint of Appeals of 1533: 'Where by dyvers sundrie old autentike histories and cronicles it is manifestly declared and expressed that this Realme of England is an Impire, and so hath been accepted in the world . . . .' (36, iii, 427) Here one finds an explicit statement of views on the nature of England, as well as practical conclusions drawn from them concerning the government of the Church. The idea that England was an 'Empire'[1] was not new: it was asserted in a letter from Cuthbert Tunstall to Henry VIII in 1517: 'But the Crown of England is an Empire of itself . . .: for which cause your Grace werith a close crown.' (110, p.225 n.2) Possibly such claims were put forward even earlier, although one can only infer them from the appearance of closed crowns on the English coinage in the reign of Henry VII.

This is found on the new coin struck by Henry, the sovereign, and, more strikingly, on the much more widely circulated groats, where the coin type with the open crown had long remained unaltered. It is likely that the motive for the new designs may have been to enhance the dignity of the King and to stress his magnificence; it is impossible to say if there was any deliberate intention of claiming additional status for him, or if this was a subsequent interpretation of the imagery. In fact, closed crowns had been employed in the fifteenth century, as early as the coronation of Henry IV, but not so regularly that the historian can assume that there was any conscious policy behind the practice.

Clearly it was in the Crown's interests to stress the unity of the country as a means of enhancing its authority. Many of the writers who specifically talked of 'England' were connected with the court either through office, such as Fortescue, or even by blood, such as Bourchier. Not all writers, however, thought in national terms; the distinguished canon lawyer William Lyndwood was not prepared to identify *patria* with *regnum*, and instead thought of it as equivalent to *regio*, which for him meant the province of Canterbury (27, p.172a). Here, expressed in ecclesiastical terms, was the distinction between North and South which recurs frequently in writings of the period. A London chronicler, writing of events in early 1461, talks of the northerners almost as if they were foreign enemies: 'it was Reported that the Quene w^t the Northern men wold come downe to the Citie and Robbe and dispoile the Citie, and distroy it vtterly, and all the Sowth Cuntre' (22, p.172). The monastic continuator of the *Croyland Chronicle* wrote of the same events in hysterical terms; the northern army moved south like a swarm of locusts, ravaging all that lay in its path. Similarly, in 1469 he speaks of the rising against Edward IV as a whirlwind coming down from the North (14, pp.531, 542).

It is hard to judge how much weight should be given to such utterances; was the designation 'northerner' intended to be purely geographical and descriptive, or did it reflect a feeling that these were men almost of a different race? One suspects that the writers were not altogether clear in their own minds; the monk of Croyland, for all his extravagant remarks about the northerners, also spoke in terms of the 'sovereignty of England', when describing a prophecy among the Welsh, whom he certainly regarded as different, that they would recover it from the English, although they failed to do so in 1469 (14, p.543). Possibly one reason for the author's attitude was his ignorance of the geography of the country; a striking instance of this is his statement that in 1461 the earl of March, whom he had rightly described as being in Wales, arrived in England having enjoyed a prosperous voyage and favoured by the west wind (14, p.532). It is perhaps hard for twentieth-century man, accustomed to consult maps for any journey, to realize how limited even an intelligent man's knowledge might be, and how gaps in his information could well be filled by colourful and confused imagination. Possibly the fact that the Robin Hood ballads, which probably took their early form in this period, seem to have had a southern origin but set their events in the North (particularly in Barnsdale, north of Doncaster, rather than in Sherwood), reflects the beliefs of southerners that the North was a strange and wild world. The northerners equally might look on the South with suspicion, or even downright hostility. During the Pilgrimage of Grace, Robert Aske talked of the northern abbeys in terms of the particular social needs of the North, and was alarmed at the prospect of their lands falling into the hands of men from the South (73, pp.34, 123). This was not new – the Dominican John Bromyard in his *Summa Predicantium* of the fourteenth century had spoken of the mutual hostility of northerners and southerners (230, p.563).

Even if one looks at the political structure of England one can see the division, and there is no doubt that political dominance was heavily weighted in favour of the South and the Midlands. The rise of the Nevilles and the Percies in the late fourteenth century was the first occasion when families of genuine northern origin came into the front rank of the nobility – one may exclude the duchy of Lancaster from any such comment, because it was closely connected with the royal family and also held substantial lands in the Midlands and the South. The Welsh Marches and the Midlands had been far more important as the power bases of major families and indeed were to remain so. The prominence of the Nevilles ended in disaster and the influence of the Percies was at best intermittent. In politics outside the magnate class one has the same picture: when one considers which boroughs were represented in fifteenth-century parliaments, one is struck by the contrasting figures from the North and the South: in Wiltshire there were sixteen boroughs and in Sussex twelve (if one includes the three Cinque Ports which fell within the shire), whereas the figures for the three northern shires of Yorkshire, Northumberland and Lancashire were three, one and none respectively. This political imbalance of North and South remained imperfectly corrected till 1832 – indeed it was to be made worse by the Tudor establishment of boroughs in the Crown duchy of Cornwall in the sixteenth century.

Yet it would be dangerous to regard such divisions as being in any way rigid. The economic crisis following the Black Death had undoubtedly given men of enterprise the opportunity to better their condition, and there was probably more mobility of population in the fifteenth century than there had been in the thirteenth. Some men may not have gone far from their original homes, but others were willing to seek their fortune at a distance: the London merchant class was recruited from every part of the country, including the far North (104, pp.210–12, 389–92). Men maintained some contact with their place of origin and might remember it in their wills. There is no surviving evidence comparable to the parish records of the seventeenth century which shows the rate of change among village inhabitants over short periods, but certainly, as we have seen (Ch.2), families died out and were replaced by others over the course of the century. There were other circumstances, too, in which men might travel about the country; knights and their retinues would go to war, merchants would pursue trade and pilgrims would travel to shrines. Margery Kempe of Lynn was perhaps exceptional in the extent of her travels, but one also remembers the *Prologue* to the *Canterbury Tales*:

> And specially, from every shires ende,
> Of Engelond, to Canterbury they wende.

In the North the shrine of St Cuthbert at Durham was second only to that of St

Thomas, although his appeal seems to have been particularly to northerners (209, pp.28–30).

A sense of nationality was not, however, incompatible with a more local loyalty, and for many members of the landed class the shire community was probably the main focus of their interests. Only occasionally did this local sentiment prove stronger than loyalty to the nation, as in 1489 when the levy of taxation for the distant Breton War led to a Yorkshire rising, in which the earl of Northumberland was murdered, and in 1497 when the Cornishmen rebelled against the payment of a subsidy for war with Scotland (73, pp.14, 15). Much work remains to be done on the structure of the shire community, and there are few shires where it has been closely analysed. A study of Cheshire in the first quarter of the fifteenth century, however, shows how the social ties of the gentry class were rooted in the locality. Families were linked by marriage alliances, and the determination of fathers to make these locally is nowhere shown more clearly than when the son of one gentleman of the shire was betrothed to the daughter of another, but the particular daughter's name was left blank in the bond of betrothal. There were also territorial ties, of lord and tenant, and of feoffees to uses and personal connections, such as those of executors. The same body of men could act as arbitrators in disputes and provide men to serve the Crown as local officials or as commissioners to levy a subsidy or array troops.

It might be argued that Cheshire was untypical: there was no great local lord, and as a palatinate jurisdiction it was specially linked to the Crown. However, the Stonor Letters suggest that the Cheshire pattern was not unique. Even a family with lands in various shires, such as the Stonors themselves, who had estates in Devon as well as their principal family holding in Oxfordshire, was closely linked by marriage to other families in its own near neighbourhood. Thomas Stonor (d.1474) was brother-in-law of Humphrey Forster of Harpeden near Henley, and father-in-law of John Barantyne of Haseley. All three of them appear quite regularly on the Oxfordshire commission of the peace. Other families who provided JPs at different times, such as the Harcourts and the Hampdens, also feature among the Stonors' correspondents (24, i, facing 7, 69–70, 113–14, 151, ii, 57–8).

The family connections of the Pastons in Norfolk do not seem to have been quite so far-reaching among the gentry families there as those of the Stonors, although Margaret Mauteby, the wife of the elder John Paston, was the daughter of another gentleman of the shire. The letters, however, show that the family was deeply involved in county affairs at a time of political turbulence, and on one occasion reveal the pride of John Paston in being a Norfolk man. In 1465 he wrote that he wished to have his doublet made of worsted 'for the worship of Norfolk' (17, iv, 188).

The community of the shire was based on a network of acquaintance and interests, and probably drew on the contacts of individuals in local government. We have seen that the Stonors and their associates served together on the Commission of the Peace, and the records of proceedings before the justices of the peace, although few in number, show how important such a group of local men was, acting along with one or two professional lawyers. Two examples will suffice to illustrate this. In Wiltshire in 1383–84, the working justices consisted of one lawyer, Sir Robert Cherleton (later Chief Justice of the Common Pleas), and four local gentry, Nicholas Bonham, Sir Philip FitzWaryn, Sir Thomas Hungerford and William de Worston. All of these men gave other service in government, as MPs, tax assessors, sheriffs, commissioners of array and so on. The Staffordshire commission of 1409–14 contained three lawyers, all active members of it, and eight gentry, who again played a part in other spheres of local government, mostly although not exclusively within the shire (31, pp.340–1, 401–2).

The extent to which a powerful magnate could dominate the shire community and act as a focus for local sentiment varied. The prominence of the duke of Norfolk in the Paston Letters reflects his local power, but the Oxfordshire of the Stonors seems to have been markedly less subject to the pre-eminence of a great man. Where there was a powerful figure, this could have important political consequences, particularly in times of civil war, as in 1471 when the Hastings connection provided important support for the newly returned Edward IV. An even more striking example of such influence was that of the Percies in Northumberland. They had been dominant there since the late fourteenth century, played an important part in Henry IV's usurpation in 1399 but were forfeited for revolt a few years later. Henry V restored them in 1416, perhaps because he hoped to use their local authority, which depended on the personal loyalty felt towards them, to safeguard his rear before further campaigns in France. Adherence to Lancaster meant a further forfeiture in 1461, but this was followed by a second restoration in 1470. Significantly, this followed the troubles in the North in the previous year, and according to one early source, the rebels then had petitioned for the earldom to be restored to the lawful heir. The most important point to note is that loyalty to such a family could survive its temporary political eclipse, and that this was rooted in the traditions of local society.

The loyalty of the North to the Percies probably reflects the more clannish nature of society in this part of the country than further south. Even when Edward IV appointed his younger brother Richard of Gloucester as his deputy in the North, the latter entered into a special indenture with Percy to define their respective powers. This system was to be the predecessor of the various experiments under the Tudors to exercise special control in the North, measures which not only reflect the problems of governing a region remote from the centre of public power but also tell us something about the tensions between a local aristocracy and the Crown. Elsewhere in the realm, in the Marches of Wales and the Principality, similar attempts were made to devolve power. Again there was a problem of lawlessness even greater than the average over the country as a whole, exacerbated by the disorders which had followed the Glyn Dŵr revolt. Men with local influence were again prominent – Edward IV relied on William Herbert, whom he made earl of Pembroke, and later on a council nominally under the prince of Wales, Richard III on his ally the duke of Buckingham, who was lord of the castle of Brecon, until the latter revolted, and Henry VII on his uncle Jasper Tudor. The first and last of these were both Welsh, (112, pp.151, 161–3) and it is likely that the element of tribal loyalty was one factor which they could employ to help in the exercise of their authority.

The establishment of such new administrative bodies in the remoter parts of the kingdom was a significant move towards building a more unified nation, but the need to create councils in the North and on the Marches is in itself an indication of how England was still divided at this date. These were only the more extreme examples of local particularism, and they were complicated by special problems, the hostile frontier in the North and the traditional privileges of the Marches in the West. Elsewhere there was no need to set up special bodies, but it is clear that much local administration had in practice to be devolved into the hands of local men.

---

1. The term 'Empire' denoted that the King owed obedience only to God and not to any temporal superior, such as the Pope or the Emperor.

CHAPTER 10

England and its neighbours

In Chapter 9, we saw that the fifteenth-century Englishman had some idea of national identity, and as being in some ways different from his neighbours. Perhaps he thought of himself more as a Kentishman or a Cornishman than as one who had something in common with men elsewhere in England, but he still distinguished Englishmen from foreigners. In the towns, one sees outbreaks of xenophobia, particularly at times of social unrest such as 1381 and 1450, when aliens were treated as scapegoats for political or economic ills. These foreigners, however, were isolated from their homelands, and more crucial for the understanding of how Britain was to develop is the consideration of how the Englishman regarded the countries closest to his own, Wales, Ireland and Scotland. Equally important was the attitude which the inhabitants of those lands had towards England.

Mental attitudes, even of individuals, are hard for the historian to ascertain, and any attempt to speak of the collective view that one nation held of another is fraught with difficulties. One may suspect that English regionalism meant that the attitude of, say, a Londoner towards the Scots was very different from that of a Northumbrian. To one, the Scot was the inhabitant of a distant land, to the other he was a potential raider who was too close for comfort. Furthermore, the relations of Wales, Ireland and Scotland to England were very different politically, and this could affect the attitudes of the ruling class to each. Since the end of the thirteenth century Wales had been subject to English rule, and remained on the whole closely bound to its larger neighbour, Ireland was divided between areas where English rule could be enforced and those where it could not, and Scotland was an independent kingdom, which had successfully resisted attempts at conquest.

If Wales possessed a sense of national identity, it owed this to its distinctive language. It had possessed no political unity at the time of the Edwardian conquest – indeed it was the very fact of its divisions which had enabled the English to carry this into effect, and unite the Principality to the kingdom by the Statute of Rhuddlan of 1284. The so-called 'Act of Union' of 1536, which will be considered later, did little more than end divisions which had persisted within Wales, and give the final blow to traditional Welsh law (110, pp.246–7). The divisions in thirteenth-century Wales had meant that political and social ties were established between English families and their Welsh neighbours, which were to persist after 1284. Edward II's Welsh officials indeed remained loyal to him against the English magnates, and later in the fourteenth and fifteenth centuries they continued to serve the Crown, even in opposition to their fellow countrymen. Even the young Owain Glyn Dŵr, later to lead a national Welsh rising, seems to have accepted the traditional friendly relationship with England, serving in the Scottish campaign of 1385, and possibly in Ireland in the 1390s. His wife was the daughter of one of the most successful Welshmen of the fourteenth century, Sir David Hanmer, who became a Justice of the King's Bench in 1383 (131, pp.22, 24, 26; 143).

Hanmer, however, was exceptional in attaining such high office, and even in Wales itself the greater administrative posts were largely filled by Englishmen, while Welshmen were limited to subordinate positions. Even more in the economic sphere there was discrimination against the native Welsh; in rural areas the settlement of Englishmen meant the transfer of the Welsh to inferior upland lands in place of their earlier more fertile valley holdings, while the towns were regarded as places for Englishmen alone. As late as 1521 ordinances were issued to prevent Welshmen becoming burgesses of Neath. Legal records also reveal the inferior status of the Welsh, most conspicuously in the term 'mere Welshmen' (*meri Wallici*), which betrays the contemptuous attitude of the English settlers. The English were privileged in court, and there were certain traditional payments which only the Welsh were liable to make, so one finds Welshmen being prepared to purchase the right to have the privileges of Englishmen (*pro libertate Anglicana habenda*) (114; 166).

The revolt of Owain Glyn Dŵr in the first decade of the fifteenth century was the greatest crisis in Anglo-Welsh relations during the later Middle Ages. It is hard to say how far this was a national rising, because Owain did not secure the support of the whole Welsh people, even at the time of his greatest military success, while there were many who deserted his cause during the English recovery (131, pp.77–80, 129–30). On the other hand, he undoubtedly attracted considerable popular support at the outbreak of the revolt, and when in 1404 he wrote to the French King as 'Owynus dei gratia princeps Wallie', he seems to have been speaking for a considerable part of his people (131, pp.35, 82–3). There is evidence for this in the support which he secured during a protracted struggle and in the difficulties which the English had in suppressing the revolt, even with some Welsh assistance, and the fact that even in defeat Owain was not betrayed to the English indicates the persistence of loyalty to him. How far he regarded himself as a national leader is hard to say – his original revolt was prompted by a private quarrel more than by national feeling, and some of his actions show little sign of being prompted by a sense of Welshness. The so-called Tripartite Indenture of 1405 between himself, Northumberland and Mortimer would have given him considerable lands in England, and the proposals to establish St Davids as a metropolitan see would have included several dioceses of western England among its suffragans (131, pp.29–31, 93–5, 120). There is, however, no doubt that during the rising he was able to exploit existing Welsh grievances.

The revolt exacerbated tension between English and Welsh. During it, the English border counties were particularly vociferous in Parliament in calling for the savage penal legislation which limited Welsh rights of office holding (112, p.148) [E], and after its suppression tests to prove Englishry were more strictly applied. As late as the 1430s, the author of the *Libelle of Englyshe Polycye* expressed a fear of further revolt in Wales (43, p.40), although there is no reason to believe that there was any serious danger of this, and this may explain why these restrictions were maintained so long. Some were relaxed by Henry VII and others removed by Henry VIII's Act of 1536. The title 'Act of Union', sometimes given to this measure is a misnomer. As its preamble makes explicit, it recognized that Wales was already incorporated with England. Its proper designation, an 'Act for Laws and Justice to be ministered in Wales in like fourme as it is in this realme', shows that its purpose was to amalgamate the legal systems of the two countries, an action which automatically removed the disabilities under which the Welsh had hitherto laboured by eliminating the legal distinctions between them and the English. It also reorganized local government in Wales, creating shires on the English pattern (36, iii, 563–9; 110, pp.253–5)

The Welsh response to Glyn Dŵr's defeat was twofold. There was certainly a tradition of resentment – fifteenth-century poetry was more bitter in tone than that of the fourteenth (143), and there was probably national sentiment behind the maintained interest in Welsh law, reflected in the survival of a considerable number of MSS of the laws of Hywel Dda, the greatest of the traditional Welsh lawgivers, from this period. Several of them contain additional notes, which show that the laws were still in practical use (166). At the same time, the fourteenth-century tradition of co-operation was restored by men who were prepared to put the past behind them and serve the English Crown. Some indeed never broke with it, such as Dafydd Gam of Brecknock, whom Henry IV ransomed from Glyn Dŵr in 1412 (112, pp.150–1; 131, p.142), and who died fighting for Henry V at Agincourt. More remarkably, the House of Tudor had been related to Glyn Dŵr and been involved in the revolt, perhaps because several of its members had served Richard II and were hostile to his supplanter; but this did not prevent Owain Tudor from entering Henry V's service and subsequently marrying his widow. Their sons, Edmund and Jasper, both became English earls, and the for-mer's son, Henry VII (110, pp.4–6). Owain was granted the legal status of an Englishman in 1432, and after rather chequered fortunes when his secret marriage was discovered, eventually died fighting for the cause of Lancaster.

The rise of the Tudors into the aristocracy resulted from their royal connec-tions; even more striking was that of the Herberts who had no such ties of blood. Sir William Herbert, created earl of Pembroke by Edward IV and given major responsibilities in the government of Wales, was of pure Welsh stock, and through his mother a grandson of Dafydd Gam. He served Richard, duke of York, after whose death he was closely connected with his son, both at his accession and during the early years of his reign. The favours conferred on him may well have been prompted by Edward IV's desire to secure Wales and to provide a focus for Welsh sentiment in opposition to the Tudors, who were the backbone of Lan-castrian resistance in Wales, where Harlech Castle held out against Herbert for a long time. Herbert's influence enabled him to bring a substantial army to Edward's support in 1469 against the forces of the northerners who had revolted at the instigation of Warwick. One chronicle source makes it clear that the Welsh element in this army was important, and that the Welshmen suffered severe cas-ualties in Herbert's defeat, and another speaks of the Welsh hoping at this time to recover the sovereignty of England which had been lost at the time of the

Anglo-Saxon invasions (14, p.543; 18, pp.6–7).

It is hard to say how far the accession of the Tudors contributed to a solution of Wales's problems. It seems clear that Henry VII, after his landing at Milford Haven, was helped by Welsh support, or at any rate neutrality, during the crucial weeks before Bosworth, and this was probably due to the sympathies evoked by contemporary Welsh bards. But he was only one-quarter Welsh, and his subsequent attitudes to Wales were more those of a practical politician, trying to exploit all his advantages in order to enforce his authority. Even in his relaxations of the penal legislation of the Glyn Dŵr period, there is no evidence of more than an attempt to govern more efficiently (110, pp.3–4, 256). Order, indeed, was hard to maintain, and it was probably the need to establish royal authority more securely that prompted Henry VIII's eventual solution in 1536.

Anglo-Welsh relations, then, show an alternation of hostility and co-operation on both sides, with the two lands finally being drawn more closely together. The main factor in this was the willingness of some of the Welsh gentry to come to terms and play an active part in government. The problem of Ireland was fundamentally different, although there were some aspects of Anglo-Irish relations which parallel conditions in Wales, such as the exclusion of the Gaelic Irish from the provisions of the common law, and from membership of mercantile and craft guilds in Dublin (133, pp.18, 44). But English rule, never so complete in Ireland as in Wales, had been severely shaken by the Bruce invasion of 1315–18, and had receded under Gaelic pressure during the fourteenth century. The key figures in Anglo-Irish relations were the aristocracy of English descent, a phenomenon which with rare exceptions did not occur in Wales. In particular, three great families, the Butler earls of Ormond and the Geraldine earls of Desmond and of Kildare, dominate the scene. These families, instead of representing a settler tradition and avoiding contact with the Irish, had a strong tendency to go native, intermarrying with the local aristocracy and following local customs (133, pp.57–8; 137, pp.18–21). The English authorities tried to enforce separation; the Statutes of Kilkenny of 1366, essentially a codification of earlier law, tried to forbid marriage alliances between the Anglo-Irish and the native Irish, to exclude the native Irish from benefices in cathedral or collegiate churches and to lay down that Irish living among the English should speak the English tongue (139, pp.291–2). These measures were ineffective, intermarriage continued and the Anglo-Irish magnates continued to pursue their interests with little reference to the distant Crown. Their control, even in Ireland, was patchy, for there were areas where the native Irish retained control and could cut communications between the lands which accepted a measure of English rule. Notably, the MacMurroughs of Leinster established a power in North Wexford and Carlow, which cut across the routes from Dublin to the south-west of the island, where the Desmonds and Ormonds held lands. This family was most powerful in the time of Art Mor MacMurrough, who died in 1416, after having been active from the time of Richard II (Ch.18), but it remained important and at feud with the English for most of the fifteenth and even into the sixteenth century (137, pp.170–1).

Endemic fighting went far to making Ireland ungovernable, and also made it financially unable to support the costs of administration and of frontier defence. The only English King to campaign there personally was Richard II, who had only short-lived success after his first visit, and both before and after his time successive Englishmen, sent over as Lieutenant or as Deputy, complained about inadequate financial provision. The story was the same from Sir William of Windsor in the fourteenth century, through Sir John Talbot under Henry V and Richard, duke of York, in the following reign, to the earl of Surrey under Henry VIII. The Anglo-Irish earl of Kildare, dominant in the 1470s, made similar complaints (133, p.65; 134, pp.9–10; 139, pp.297–307, 350–1, 381, 396). The English government had various expedients in its Irish policy, notably reliance on English magnates whose territorial interests in Ireland gave them some incentive to act firmly; one thinks particularly of successive members of the House of Mortimer under Richard II and again in 1423–25. All died in Ireland, although only one in battle. The duke of York, appointed Lieutenant in 1447, also inherited lands from the Mortimers. He was able to turn his power in Ireland to advantage in English domestic politics, fleeing for refuge there in 1459 after defeat at Ludford Bridge (Ch.23). Under his influence the Irish Parliament affirmed in 1460 that 'the land of Ireland is and at all times has been corporate of itself . . . freed of the burden of any special law of the realm of England' (139, pp.313–15, 334–6, 362–3, 378–87). This declaration was made by an assembly which represented the Anglo-Irish rather than the Gaelic Irish – the native population was unrepresented in Parliament until Henry VIII raised certain of the Gaelic chiefs to the peerage (133, p.33).

Native Ireland stood apart from events in England, although it might come to terms with the Anglo-Irish, who, equally with the Gaelic Irish, resented interference from across the sea. For much of the time, however, it went its own way; the native Brehon law did not begin to retreat until the sixteenth century, and the greatest of the native Irish lived in a society which was little touched by the normal customs of the rest of Christendom, even as late as the reign of Elizabeth. Native law did not distinguish between legitimate and illegitimate children, which meant that in practice marriage customs were secular and polygamous. Philip Maguire, lord of Fermanagh, who died in 1395, had twenty sons by eight different mothers, and the second earl of Clanrickard, who died in 1582, was survived by at least five of his six wives (137, pp.11, 49, 74). These native lords shared political aims with the Anglo-Irish magnates, essentially the limitation of English rule from Dublin, and as only one of the three great Anglo-Irish families, the Ormonds, had significant interests in England, it was natural that the Kildares and the Desmonds should be prepared to establish connections with Gaelic society.

Ormond support for the Lancastrians probably explains why Edward IV had assistance from Kildare and Desmond, and it was certainly this Lancastrian sympathy which led to the exile of the earl and the eclipse of the family in the third quarter of the fifteenth century. At the same time the Desmonds went increasingly native, leaving the House of Kildare politically dominant in Anglo-Irish society. Its power excited hostility and apprehension, and one sees an alternation of members of the family holding the key offices in Irish government with their opposition to anyone else who was entrusted with power. It would be fair to say that the Crown could not govern effectively without the support of the family, but dared not rely on it completely. The seventh, eighth and ninth earls effectively dominated Ireland until the 1530s. Their power was based on land (and early in the sixteenth century the grant to the eighth earl of all lands which he could recover from rebels strengthened this), but they were also connected through marriage with a number of Gaelic and Anglo-Irish families (133, pp.155–6).

Ireland did not affect English politics as much as Wales did, and it is significant that English writers say little about Irish affairs. Presumably the reason was its greater remoteness, and the lack of interest of most Englishmen in it, apart perhaps from the traders of the west coast ports such as Bristol, who bought fish, hides and timber in exchange of iron, salt and cloth (94, pp.191–201). Its main political role was its support for the House of York from 1459 onwards – as we have seen, the Irish Parliament of 1460 asserted its independence of England at a time of Lancastrian dominance, and in 1470, when Henry VI recovered the throne, Kildare held Ireland in the name of Edward IV (139, pp.394–5). After 1485, this loyalty to York took the form of supporting the pretenders, Lambert Simnel in 1487 and to a lesser extent Perkin Warbeck in 1491 (139, pp.403, 406). It was significantly just after this that one sees the strongest series of measures taken in the fifteenth century to bring Ireland under control, those taken, during a period when the Kildares were out of favour, by Sir Edward Poynings, the recently appointed Lord Deputy, in 1495. His Parliament legislated that the chief officers of Ireland should hold their posts solely at the King's will and pleasure, annulled the 1460 Act which made it treason to attack any person in Ireland under an English seal, and declared that the English seals were to be obeyed in Ireland. Its most famous enactment restricted the Irish Parliament – none was to be held until the King and the English Parliament had approved its proposed acts and a royal licence had been obtained for its summons. Another Act of the same Parliament provided that statutes made within England should apply in Ireland (133, pp.177–8).

These measures played a considerable part in establishing the governmental framework of Anglo-Irish relations for the next three centuries, although relations between Gaelic Ireland and the Anglicized areas were to be further complicated by the plantation of new immigrants at the turn of the sixteenth and seventeenth centuries. The policy pursued in the late Middle Ages, of establishing an area of English law, the so-called Pale, reflects the defensive attitude of the English to the Gaelic areas, and this seems to have become more pronounced during the fifteenth century. Although effective government had been limited to the areas near Dublin since early in the century, Poynings took steps to define the Pale more precisely, organizing a defence system, with a warning system of fires on various hills. This is a clear sign that he felt it was impossible to control the whole island and that much of it would have to be allowed to go its own way. Such a solution could satisfy no one, and left the island in a politically unstable condition, where power could rest only with those strong enough to take it by force (133, pp.132–3, 175).

If Wales was largely incorporated under English rule and Ireland precariously poised between control and independence, England's third neighbour within the

British Isles, Scotland, was politically distinct. Like Ireland, it comprised two nations, but by the late Middle Ages effective authority centred on the Lowland areas, which were linguistically, and hence culturally, closer to England than was either Ireland or Wales. In the Highland areas there were many parallels with Gaelic Ireland, with clan chiefs who paid little heed to a king in the South, or who negotiated alliances with the English King against their own ruler, but it was possible for the Scottish Crown to take some measures against them with at least limited success, and they never played so prominent a part in national affairs as did the Lowland magnates.

The accession of Robert the Steward to the Scottish throne in 1371 marked the achievement of independence against the attempts of Edward III to overthrow the settlement of 1328. Neither support for Edward Balliol, who ultimately surrendered his claims to the English King in 1356, the captivity of David II and the subsequent ransom treaty, nor a proposal in 1364 that Edward should succeed the childless David, had led to the surrender of Scottish independence (138, pp.161, 163, 193). The English did not entirely abandon their claims of overlordship, which were certainly resurrected in 1400 (possibly after a tactless letter in which Robert III addressed Henry IV as duke of Lancaster), and were probably reasserted by Henry V during the unsuccessful negotiations in 1416 for the release of James I from captivity in England. In the debates on nationality at the Council of Constance in 1417, the English claimed that the Scots were part of the English nation, along with Wales and four kingdoms in Ireland, although they do not seem to have made any specific reference to the claims of overlordship (132). Although Edward IV reasserted the claim to sovereignty in 1481, accusing James III of neglecting to do homage and affirming his intention of restoring the exiled earl of Douglas (138, p.491), this should probably be regarded as a tactical move to attract support from possible opponents of the Scottish King. Probably no English king after Edward III seriously hoped to secure rights of overlordship; it is noteworthy that no attempt was made to enforce it in the eventual ransom negotiations for James I in 1424. The effective abandonment of the claim was probably due to the fact that the English kings were more concerned with ambitions in France or were absorbed in internal faction.

Anglo-Scottish relations were not therefore affected by the tensions, found in Wales and Ireland, created by a conquest and the existence of an alien ruling class. It is not easy to obtain a clear picture of the attitudes which each nation had to the other – Scottish records and chronicles are sparse, and there are surprisingly few comments on the Scots in English writings, probably because the great bulk of the latter came from the largely indifferent south of the country. There is clearer evidence of hostility in the North; although one may discount descriptions of the Scots in the York civic records as 'enemys and rebells' and 'auncient enemys' as statements made in time of war, one cannot disregard the sentiments expressed in legal cases when a man's nationality had been questioned. In 1477, a time of peace between the two countries, there were two such: John Colyn complained that he 'was diffamyd of the chylder of iniquite be veray malesse, that he shud be a Skotte and no Ynglysman', and John Saunderson showed 'how that he of late ayanest right and gude conscience by the children of wekydness was wrongfully noysed, slaundered and defamed that he should be a Scotisheman'. Hostility to the Scots cannot, however, have been sufficient to exclude them entirely from England; not only do these cases presuppose that a man living in York might be a Scot, but also in 1480, when war was imminent, some fifty Scots resident in England sought and obtained letters of denization, so as to avoid the risk of having their property confiscated (138, p.490).

The Scots reciprocated this hostility. Aeneas Sylvius Piccolomini, later Pope Pius II, who visited Scotland in the 1430s, commented that nothing pleased the Scots more than abuse of the English (138, p.297). Walter Bower, the abbot of Inchcolm, took time in his *Scotichronicon* to reiterate the old slander against the English that they were born with tails. There was a patriotic tradition in literature, voiced in Barbour's *Bruce* in the fourteenth century and Blind Harry's *Wallace* in the fifteenth; indeed there was in the latter at least implicit criticism of the policy of *rapprochement* with England being pursued by James III. The whole corpus of ballad literature from the border areas reflects traditions of hostility, and shows how deeply they were reflected in folk memory, even although the lateness of the texts makes their value slight as a detailed source for events. Nor was it only the ballad writers who voiced such sentiments. Skelton, whose background may have been north country, was vitriolic in his attacks on the Scots, with his savage poem on Flodden and his sneering 'How the douty Duke of Albany, lyke a cowarde knyght, ran away shamfully', which probably refers to an unsuccessful Scottish raid in 1522. When, after Flodden, George Dundas reiterated the story about Englishmen with tails, Skelton retorted savagely in macaronic verse.

Yet literary evidence also shows the existence of a Scottish attraction to England. In his *Lament for the Makars* William Dunbar began his melancholy roll-call of the dead with 'the noble Chawcer, of Makaris flouir' and followed him with two other Englishmen, Gower and Lydgate. The Chaucerian tradition of writing was influential in fifteenth-century Scotland, notably in Robert Henryson but even, in some stylistic techniques, in Blind Harry. Admittedly, Dunbar was Anglophil, writing in praise of London, and, as a court poet, commemorating the marriage of James IV and Margaret Tudor. Nor were literary connections confined to the poets. In 1521 John Major, one of the leading Scots scholars of his day, wrote his *History of Greater Britain*, in which he affirmed that while there were two kingdoms in the island, the Scottish and the English, the inhabitants were all Britons, He was even eirenical on the question of tails, considering that while Englishmen had had them in the past, they no longer were so encumbered. Major's attitude to the English is all the more striking because he had spent much of his working life in France and might have been expected to stress Scotland's ancient alliance with that country.

Ultimately, however, only political moves could draw the two countries together. Although in the third quarter of the fifteenth century each country provided a refuge for rebels and exiles from the other, such as the Lancastrians in Scotland and the Douglases in England, the end of this period sees a move to peace. In the 1470s, when James III's domestic political position was fairly strong, he took steps towards two marriage alliances between the two countries. In 1474 his son, aged not quite two, was betrothed to Edward IV's five-year-old daughter, and in 1479 there were negotiations for the marriage of the King's sister to Edward's brother-in-law, Earl Rivers. One might note the preamble to the 1474 treaty: 'Forsmuche as this noble isle called Grete Britaigne canne not be kepte and mainteigned better in welthe and prosperite than such things to be practized and concluded betwene the kyngs of both reames, England and Scotland, whereby thaye and thair subgetts might be assured to lyve in peas. . . .' (138, pp.478–9, 487–9) In fact the negotiations came to nothing; when it turned out that James's sister was pregnant by William, Lord Crichton, Edward protested his outraged honour and annulled the earlier betrothal also. The initiative in these negotiations seems to have come largely from James, who may have been hoping for English neutrality while he dealt with his own troublesome subjects. Edward was less enthusiastic, although originally he was probably pleased to secure his northern frontier before invading France in 1475.

Although this proposed marriage for the Scottish prince was unsuccessful, he was eventually (nearly thirty years later as James IV) to marry another English princess. He made marriage with a daughter of Henry VII a prior condition for peace and friendship with England; this was agreed in 1502 and the marriage was celebrated in the following year (138, pp.553–4). Peace lasted until Henry VII's death, but his son was less disposed to be friendly towards the Scots. In the early years of his reign his ambitions in Europe led to a renewal of the Franco-Scottish alliance, and to the disastrous invasion of England which culminated at Flodden in 1513. Even after this, however, there were still some Scottish lords who looked for closer friendship with England rather than to the old association with France. This division in foreign policy was important for nearly half a century, down to 1560, but did not become crucial until the minority of Mary and the regency of her French mother. Many of the early moves towards the formation of a pro-English party in Scotland were little more than the old tendency for men at odds with the existing government to seek help south of the border (116, p.36), and the period when such a group became really influential lies beyond the scope of this volume. A hundred years after the marriage of 1503, the failure of the Tudor line gave the English throne to a Scottish king, and created a personal union of the two kingdoms.

So far we have considered the relations of England with its neighbours. How did the Welsh, Irish and Scots regard each other? There are some indications that they not only appreciated their common interest in resisting England but also felt themselves to be in some sense kindred. In November 1401 Owain Glyn Dŵr wrote for help to the Irish chiefs and to Robert III of Scotland, although his letters were intercepted and never reached their proposed destinations. To the former he wrote that ancient prophecies said that Irish help would be necessary for this triumph, and (more practically) that war in Wales would free Ireland from English intervention (131, pp.46–7). He also claimed kinship with the Scots, one of whom, the chronicler Bower, noted the Welsh struggle sympathetically. Scottish interest in Ireland persisted after the Bruce campaigns failed in 1318: in the mid fifteenth century the barony of the Glens of Antrim was acquired by Donald Balloch, a kinsman of the lord of the Isles, and in 1481 James III tried to rouse the native Irish against England in retaliation for Edward IV's intrigues with the restive MacDonalds (138, pp.362, 495). More striking, because there was no political pressure behind it, was the fact that when the University of Glasgow was founded in the mid fifteenth century, provision was made to include Irish students in one of its nations, Rothesay. In fact the numbers of Irish recorded were small, but there were a few, drawn from the Gaelic areas, despite the fact that much of Scotland was no longer Gaelic in character.

England's relations with its neighbours in the late Middle Ages saw some breaking down of the old barriers with Wales and Scotland. The lifting of restrictions on the Welsh was gradual, but despite them, Welshmen began to play a part in English political life. It is at least symbolically significant that Henry VII was of Welsh descent in the paternal line. Anglo-Scottish distrust, although always latent and liable to flare up into open hostility, was perhaps less profound than in the early fourteenth century, and some men at any rate saw that both countries had some interests in common. Possibly a crucial factor here was the loss by the English kings of their French lands. This made them rather more concerned with insular affairs, and as the English were less inclined to assert claims in France, the French paid less heed to maintaining an alliance, of which the main value had been to provide a diversion in the North. It is significant that the periods of Anglo-Scottish *rapprochement* in the 1470s and around 1500 coincide with times when the English kings were not particularly aggressive in Europe. Even Edward IV's campaign of 1475 must be regarded more as a demonstration than as a real attempt to recover lost lands. England's less happy relations with Ireland show that tension there was maintained, with the Irish, both Gaelic and Anglo-Irish, being forced into subordination to an alien government in Dublin. The attempt to incorporate Gaelic Ireland, through its chiefs, into one nation with the Anglo-Irish lies beyond our period, but it may well have been doomed from the start by the attitudes which had developed in the fifteenth century and earlier. Once this bitterness had been created, it was arguably impossible for later attempts to solve the Irish question to have much chance of success.

CHAPTER 11

The monarchy

Between 1370 and 1530 ten kings occupied the English throne, with the reigns of eight of them falling completely within the period. Of these eight, three (Richard II, Henry VI and Edward V) were deposed and subsequently came to violent ends, a fourth (Richard III) died in battle defending his title and a fifth (Edward IV) lost the throne for a time but subsequently recovered it. Furthermore, Richard II may have been temporarily deposed in December 1387, only to be restored for another dozen years when his enemies failed to agree on a successor, and Henry IV, Henry V and Henry VII all survived attempts to overthrow them by force. As far as the monarchy was concerned, this was a period of unequalled instability in English history, as can be seen when one looks both at earlier and at later times. Between 1066 and 1370, only Edward II had come to a violent end following a rebellion, and even John and Henry III, who had faced armed insurrections, were able to retain the throne till the ends of their lives. After 1530, only Charles I (unless one also includes Lady Jane Grey among English monarchs) was to be put to death, while James II lost the Crown by flight. The average length of each reign in this period was also markedly shorter than those before or after, a further sign of the monarchy's weakness. The most obvious problem, therefore, for the historian is why at this time the monarchy was so insecure.

The exceptional instability was partly fortuitous. The personalities of some kings contributed to their downfall, because the standing of the monarchy could not be totally separated from the individual who was king at the time, although there were certain functions of monarchy, as will be shown later, which had to be regarded as institutional rather than personal. The fact that all three kings who were ultimately deposed succeeded as minors, Henry VI as a baby and the other two before entering their teens, was probably important in only one case, that of Edward V, who was unable to defend his inheritance against his uncle Richard, duke of Gloucester, at a time when magnate rivalries were acute (Ch.25). His reign lasted for less than three months, but both Richard II and Henry VI survived minority, and it was their adult conduct which was to lead to their eventual destruction.

Richard II undoubtedly gave offence by his ambitions for the royal prerogative and the capricious arbitrariness of his conduct. This was apparent both in his political actions against his enemies (Ch.18) and in the way in which he and his advisers tried to extend the scope of the law of treason beyond that of the common law and the normal courts. Thus in 1390, the Court of Chivalry was given power to judge matters arising out of war within the realm, which could not be determined by the common law, while in Haxey's case (1397), the King persuaded the lords to declare that anyone who should excite the Commons to reform any matter touching the King's person, government or regality should be held a traitor. It is significant also that it was in Richard's reign that the term 'high treason' came into use for the first time (36, ii, 69; 161, pp.114, 137, 229). Actions such as these left Richard politically isolated in the face of the rebellion of his cousin Henry of Lancaster. In Henry VI's case, his political ineptitude was manifest long before his deposition, even indeed before his first attack of insanity posed further problems for the government of the realm (Ch.22).

Indeed, despite the instability of the monarchy at this period, it is striking how reluctant the nobility were to overthrow the King. It took a great deal of misgovernment before they would venture on so drastic a step. During the minorities of both Richard II and Henry VI, and while the latter was insane, their titles were not challenged, and the great men of the realm took steps to ensure that government would be properly conducted. No adult king was deprived of his title except as a last resort. when he had lost so much support that a rival could win the realm by force. Edward IV's temporary loss of the throne in 1470 and the overthrow of Richard III in 1485, some two years after his usurpation, both occurred when a substantial proportion of the nobility had been alienated from the Crown.

In the legal thought of the thirteenth and fourteenth centuries there was what was called a doctrine of royal capacities, whereby a distinction was drawn between the King as a person and the King as a ruler. It was to the latter that baronial loyalty was due, and it was regarded as lawful to take action against a king who failed to fulfil his obligations. Although there are still traces of this concept in fifteenth-century writings, these tended to be few, and royal authority was held to be indistinguishable from the person of the King (161, pp.98–9). A clear sign of this is to be found in the changing attitude to the offence called 'accroachment' (or usurpation) of the royal power. Numerous cases of this occurred in the early fourteenth century, but in 1388 the magnates, in revolt against Richard II and the court faction, charged the King's favourites with this crime, and the lords in Parliament declared that this was treasonable. Now there is no doubt that the accused had been acting in accordance with the King's wishes, so their actions could be regarded as treason only if the Crown were held to be distinct from the person of the King (161, pp.62–74, 96). In 1397 Richard had these sentences reversed, thereby implicitly denying that such actions could be treasonable, and it is significant that accroachment declined as a charge during the fifteenth century, not only against royal favourites but generally. The charge of compassing the King's death became more normal in prosecutions initiated by the Crown, and in the most noteworthy magnate attack on a royal favourite. that against Suffolk in 1450, the term 'accroachment' did not appear (161, pp.96–8). The civil wars of the late fifteenth century, and the alternation of tenure of the throne between Lancastrian and Yorkist kings did serve to restore the doctrine of capacities in certain circumstances: in Edward IV's reign a legal suit was brought by a man who had obtained letters of denization from Henry VI, and the question was raised whether the denization were lawful, because if it were not, the plaintiff would have no title to sue. The judges upheld the validity of the letters, and therefore that there was a possible distinction between a king *de facto* and a king *de iure* (161, pp.99–100). This must, however, be seen more as a means of solving a technical issue in the administration of the law rather than as a pronouncement on the nature of the royal title.

The possiblity of a genuine conflict of allegiance, as between 'right' and 'possession' was indeed a major problem, and one which contributed to the instability of the monarchy, because the law of succession was itself unclear. Since the accession of Henry III in 1216, the Crown had passed without dispute by male primogeniture, because there had always been a male heir of the direct line. In the twelfth century the accession of Henry II had represented the principle that a right to the Crown could be transmitted by a woman, and that of John had shown that a direct heir could be set aside. When Edward III laid claim to the French throne, this presupposed a belief in the right of a claim being transmitted through the female line, against the Valois assertion of the validity of claims through the male line only. But there is no doubt that there was in the fourteenth century a general tendency to stress the rights of male descent; not only were the French succession disputes of 1316 and 1328 settled in favour of the male heir, but in 1373 an attempt at defining the Scottish succession by the first of the Stewart kings had pronounced in favour of the male line, despite his own inheritance of it through his mother. (Ultimately, of course, this ruling was disregarded in the succession of Mary in 1542.) Even in England, there was in the fourteenth century a tendency for estates and titles to be entailed in the male line and for the claims of females to be set aside. The problem was not resolved if this procedure was to apply to the Crown as well as to lesser dignities (88, p.273; 138, p.183).

The most articulate of fifteenth-century legal writers on constitutional matters, Chief Justice Fortescue, was originally a Lancastrian partisan, and wrote in defence of the Lancastrian title, but later (after the Yorkist victory) retracted his views and admitted that the estate of the Crown was something too great for him to make any pronouncement on the matter. In this he was repeating the view expressed by himself and the other judges in 1460 when Richard, duke of York, laid claim to the throne and they were required to give their views on this subject (165, pp.22–3). At no stage did any clear legal decision on the succession secure general acquiescence, and the history of the Crown during much of this period shows that it was political power rather than any theoretical right which determined who was to obtain the throne. Successful contenders would seek to buttress their title by formulating claims of greatly varying plausibility.

The long-term problem of the succession may have lain behind some of the tensions of the 1376 Parliament, for although the death of the Black Prince while it was in session left an undoubted heir in his son Richard, the succession after Richard was uncertain. Was the next heir, Edward III's third son, John of Gaunt, the leader of the court faction, or the daughter of his late second son, Lionel of Clarence, Philippa, wife of Edmund Mortimer, earl of March, who was the leading magnate opposed to the court? [B.1] Parliament's recognition of Richard as his grandfather's heir may reflect suspicion that Gaunt already had designs on the throne, although his moderate actions on Edward III's death, when he did not even claim a formal standing as first among the young King's councillors, suggests that popular hostility to him, on this point at least, was unjustified. When Richard became king, it was presumably hoped that the succession problem would be resolved when he married and had an heir, but when his marriage remained child-less, the issue became more acute. One chronicle source suggests that the young earl of March, who succeeded his father in 1381, was formally recognized as heir; there is no official record surviving to support this, but although it is true that the writer shows considerable confusion at this point in his work (198, iii, 396 n.1), he may be reflecting popular gossip on the succession question. Seven years younger than Richard, March was too young to be politically important until the 1390s, and then it was largely in Ireland where he had lands that he was most active, being left as Lieutenant after Richard's expedition in 1395. When he was killed in 1398, his son was only six, so it may well have been his premature death which brought about a Lancastrian rather than a Mortimer succession in 1399. In the late 1390s Richard does not appear to have been particularly concerned about who was to follow him – as he was only thirty-two at the time of his dep-osition, he was perhaps hoping to live long enough to have an heir by his second wife, even although she was still only a child. His jealousy towards March, who had been popularly welcomed at the Shrewsbury Parliament in January 1398, and March's dismissal from the Irish lieutenancy later in the year before the news of his death reached England, may reflect a feeling that the man with the strongest reversionary title to the throne was a potential focus of discontent (150, pp.206–7).

In 1399 Henry of Lancaster had little option but to remove Richard from the throne, as the latter's revenge in 1397 against the Appellants, his opponents of a decade earlier, had shown that he had a long memory for grievances (Ch.18). But while many of the magnates might countenance a deposition and indeed might be relieved at it, it was less certain that they would acquiesce in a usurpation by Henry. The Percies, his most powerful allies in the North, must have been more sympathetic to a Mortimer claim, as the earl of Northumberland's son Hot-spur was married to a sister of the late earl of March. One may wonder if their support for the deposition may have been prompted by the hope that the young earl might succeed. The whole course of events in 1399 shows that the title to the throne was uncertain; undoubtedly Henry concealed his aims from friend and foe alike until he could build up his military strength and play on popular favour. Chief Justice Thirnyng opposed any claim to the throne based on conquest, and a committee of Parliament rejected as false the story that he was lawful heir by descent from Henry III through Edmund Crouchback, allegedly superseded by his brother Edward I. Henry's attempt to employ such a cock-and-bull story illus-trates the weakness of his hereditary claim, and might indeed suggest that he recognized the superiority of a Mortimer title, because he made no attempt to assert his undoubted status as the heir male of Edward III. After Richard's abdication, Henry claimed the throne 'challenging this realm of England', in vir-tue of his descent from Henry III and through God's grace, which had helped him to recover it, when it was suffering from 'default of governance and undoing of the good laws' (135, pp.52–4). The word 'challenge' is important, because it implies that Henry was putting forward a claim, which rested on the idea of the judgement of God in battle, and was not basing his title on any form of parlia-